ASK FOR

MORE

10 Questions to Negotiate Anything

Alexandra Carter

SIMON & SCHUSTER

New York   London   Toronto   Sydney   New Delhi

Simon & Schuster
1230 Avenue of the Americas
New York, NY 10020

First Simon & Schuster hardcover edition May 2020

Names and some identifying details of the people referred to in
this book by first name only have been changed.

SIMON & SCHUSTER and colophon are registered trademarks of Simon & Schuster, Inc.

For information about special discounts for bulk purchases, please contact
Simon & Schuster Special Sales at 1-866-506-1949 or business@simonandschuster.com.

The Simon & Schuster Speakers Bureau can bring authors to your live event.
For more information or to book an event contact the
Simon & Schuster Speakers Bureau at 1-866-248-3049 or
visit our website at www.simonspeakers.com.

Interior design by Ruth Lee-Mui

Manufactured in the United States of America

1 3 5 7 9 10 8 6 4 2

Library of Congress Cataloging-in-Publication Data
Names: Carter, Alexandra, author.
Title: Ask for more : 10 questions to negotiate anything / Alexandra Carter.
Description: New York : Simon & Schuster, 2020. | Includes bibliographical references and index.
Identifiers: LCCN 2019051712 (print) | LCCN 2019051713 (ebook) | ISBN 9781982130480
(hardcover) | ISBN 9781982130497 (paperback) | ISBN 9781982130503 (ebook)
Subjects: LCSH: Negotiation
Classification: LCC BF637.N4 C368 2020 (print) | LCC BF637.N4 (ebook) |
DDC 302.3—dc23
LC record available at https://lccn.loc.gov/2019051712
LC ebook record available at https://lccn.loc.gov/2019051713
ISBN 978-1-9821-3048-0
ISBN 978-1-9821-3050-3 (ebook)

To Greg and Caroline—
I couldn't ask for more.

CONTENTS

INTRODUCTION

We make our world significant by the courage of our
questions and by the depth of our answers.
—CARL SAGAN

What made you pick up this book?

Perhaps you want to negotiate more or feel more comfortable doing it. You'd like to negotiate for a promotion or a raise—or both. You want to feel confident asking for what you're worth.

Perhaps you're an entrepreneur and want to grow your business. You'd like to create more loyal clients and get more value from your deals. Maybe you're contemplating a career transition and want to find your calling.

Or perhaps the reason you picked this book up has nothing to do with work. You've been in conflict with someone, and it's eating up your mental energy. You'd like more understanding in your relationships.

Whatever you're facing, you now hold in your hands the tool to help you break through: Ten questions that will help you negotiate anything.

It might seem counterintuitive to learn how to negotiate by asking questions. Twenty years ago, before I first studied conflict resolution, I assumed that negotiation meant winning points, or making demands. But two decades later, I've learned something remarkably simple from having

1

resolved hundreds of conflicts as a trained mediator: you get more value in negotiation by asking than you do from arguing.

When you ask the right questions, of yourself and others, you open a window to create value far beyond what you can imagine. Leading your negotiation with questions not only helps your bottom line, but it helps you connect to people in a way that can transform relationships, personally and professionally.

When you change your questions, you change the conversation. In this book, we'll discuss the power of questions—and not just any questions, but open questions. An open question can become your new negotiation tool to unlock deals and possibilities.

Asking for more also means you start negotiations at the beginning—with you. The first negotiation in any situation is the one you have with yourself. When you spend time asking yourself questions first, before sitting down with someone else, you'll get more value and more enjoyment from the negotiation process and be more prepared. I'll walk you through the questions to ask yourself so that you can walk into any negotiation with confidence.

Finally, this book will change the way you think about negotiation itself. Ever read a negotiation book and think, *That's not me*? Think again. I'm going to give you a new definition of what it means to negotiate, one that takes negotiation beyond corporate boardrooms and politicians trading soundbites and into everyday life—where we work, live, and dream. One that's more about listening than performing. One that allows you to be yourself while also creating more value out of every interaction you have. One that takes you far beyond a handshake and helps you create a lifetime of value.

Asking for More from Negotiation

Too often, we are taught that negotiation means talking instead of asking. Making your arguments. Controlling the conversation. That negotiation means having all the answers and getting your way to prevent the other person from getting their way. And if we do ask questions, we should only ask questions to which we already know the answer.

This performative concept of negotiation not only turns a lot of people off, leading them to avoid it, but it's also ineffective. You don't prepare to become an expert negotiator by looking in the mirror and rehearsing your arguments. That's not negotiation—that's public speaking. And when you sit down with someone else and lead with those arguments, the other person is less likely to hear you, and prone to give what you say much less credit.

Having worked with thousands of negotiators over the course of my career, I can tell immediately who the experts in the room are. Expert negotiators know that their greatest source of strength in negotiation is not bluster but *knowledge*. Expert negotiation requires you to understand yourself and someone else well enough to conduct a conversation that produces value for both parties. But most people don't ask the right questions to acquire that knowledge. Research shows that only 7 percent of people ask good questions in negotiation—even when sharing information about themselves, or getting the right information about their counterpart, could greatly benefit them. If you start negotiating by launching into your arguments, or asking the wrong questions, you not only miss the chance to create understanding across the table, you may end up settling for less.

But it doesn't have to be that way.

What Is Negotiation?

When I set out to write this book, I surveyed hundreds of people from many professions and more than a dozen countries about their definition of negotiation, with a sneaking suspicion that most would have negative connotations around the word. In fact, many of the people who answered the survey defined it as something akin to "a back-and-forth discussion to get to an agreement," with half using the words "compromise" or "concession"—which mean, in effect, a *loss*. For the people we surveyed, negotiation was analogous to giving up or giving in.

In other words, most people see negotiation as something you do only when you're trying to get a specific result. And that you have to lose something when you do it.

Everywhere we turn, whether in a dictionary or a book or on a television show, you get a similar picture. People arguing politics or trading numbers, to try and reach an agreement. For example, some dictionary definitions include:

- Formal discussions in which people or groups try to reach an agreement, especially in a business or political situation. (*Macmillan*)
- A formal discussion between people who have different aims or intentions, especially in business and politics, during which they try to reach an agreement. (*Collins*)

As a result, we are taught to think about negotiation in a limited way that excludes most people and problems. Is it really only negotiation if you're trading numbers or political positions? Is negotiation really just the back-and-forth immediately preceding an agreement or contract?

Negotiation: A New Definition

When I teach people to negotiate, I start by putting up a point-of-view picture of a kayak going through a series of sea caves. You see the front of the boat, the paddle, some clear blue water, and several caves ahead. I ask: "What does this have to do with negotiation?" Most people look at the picture and say things like, "Negotiation is about strategic decisions. You need to pick which cave you want," or "Negotiation means choosing the best of the options in front of you." "Negotiation is advocating for the result you want."

This is a pretty narrow, outcome-focused way to talk about negotiation. My conception of negotiation comes from a different definition, the one that's way down the list when you open the dictionary:

Negotiate /v/: to successfully travel along or over (*Merriam-Webster*)

When you negotiate a kayak through sea caves, or negotiate your way along a hiking trail—in other words, when you *successfully travel* in the direction you need to go—what are you doing? You're *steering*. In my work, I teach that *negotiation is any conversation in which you are steering a relationship*.

I love the kayak metaphor because it illustrates so many things about negotiation. How do you steer in a kayak? You have to paddle consistently. Even if all you want to do is continue on the course you've set, you still need a steady rhythm, left and right, in order to continue traveling the way you want to go. What happens to a kayak if we stop steering? We keep moving, but maybe not in the direction we want. Outside forces like the wind and water will carry us away. And the kayak metaphor tells us one more thing about negotiation: You need the right information to steer with accuracy. You can't close your eyes and ears and expect to arrive at your destination. You need to watch the waves and feel the direction of the wind. Everything you see, hear, and feel helps you steer with accuracy toward your goal.

All of us can benefit from steering more consistently, and with better information—but too often we don't. Because we've been taught that negotiation is only when you're talking about money, or that it's for politicians or businesspeople, we often quit steering. We put the paddle down and wait until our once-a-year salary negotiation, or until we feel like we're in crisis. And sometimes we *are* steering, but we steer haphazardly because we don't have the right information to help us plot our destination.

So what happens when you treat negotiation like steering a kayak? First, it means you don't wait until the contract comes up to negotiate with your boss or client. You don't wait until your relationship feels like it is in crisis to have a conversation. Instead, you are continuously piloting those relationships in every conversation you have. And second, you take in the right information to help you steer toward your goal. You ask great questions. You use advanced listening skills to get information that helps you shape your deals. In sum, you approach those conversations intentionally. You treat them all as part of your *negotiation of that relationship*.

When you've been steering your relationship consistently, you'll get even better results when you do need to talk about money, or clients, or who forgot to sign the kids up for summer camp. The result is not only more deals—and more advantageous deals—but stronger relationships that produce value far beyond money.

A Different Approach to Negotiation

If this doesn't sound like your typical approach to negotiation, you're right. I've always thought about negotiation differently, and I think it goes back to the way I first learned it. While a student at Columbia Law School, I learned negotiation backward—meaning I studied mediation first. What's the difference between the two? While negotiation involves advocating for what you want, mediation is a process in which an outside third person helps two or more people negotiate with each other in order to reach a mutually beneficial goal. The mediator doesn't take anyone's side or feed the negotiating parties the right answer. Instead, she helps people raise the right questions to see the bigger picture of their situation more clearly; in doing so, she helps them negotiate with more accuracy and find more hidden value than they might on their own. Most people in my field study mediation *after* negotiation (if they study mediation at all), so they miss out on the mediation skills that could make them even better negotiators.

Over the last fifteen years, I have been that mediator, that outside third person for thousands of people, helping them negotiate toward their goals. From that neutral chair, I've seen clearly how the me-first, argumentative approach many people took to negotiation repeatedly backfired in the sessions playing out in front of me. I also started to see a negotiation approach that really worked. Much of what I did as a mediator was listening and asking good questions of both people in the room—and when the negotiators learned how to do that for themselves, they achieved the best results.

So when I teach negotiation, my goal is to teach it in a way that helps everyone—not just businesspeople and politicians—know that they, too, are negotiators. Whoever you are, and whatever you do, the questions in this book will help you negotiate anything. And you'll learn to do it in a way that takes you far beyond one handshake to experience some of the magic—the added value, clarity, understanding, personal transformation—I've helped thousands of people achieve in mediation.

This is the *more* in *Ask for More*.

What's the Best Way to Steer?

To steer effectively, you need to see, hear, and understand where you're going. One of the most senior diplomats at the United Nations, Assistant Secretary-General Nikhil Seth, shared with me that the old tools of negotiation and diplomacy—where you hold your cards to the vest and then try to spring a surprise on your adversary—no longer work. In this age, where so much information can travel around the world with the stroke of a keyboard, it's much harder to surprise an adversary. Instead, he finds the key to negotiation is transparency: getting and sharing the right information.

Recent research on negotiation and leadership bears that out. The best negotiators and leaders are the ones who ask the right questions and therefore get the right information to help them make better deals.

But achieving transparency is a lot harder than it seems in this age of information overload. We struggle to tune out internet chatter, other people's opinions, even our own expectations, and truly see ourselves for who we are and what we need. And when we struggle to see ourselves, we inevitably fail to see the people around us—our clients, colleagues, spouses, and adversaries. This lack of perspective leads to all kinds of challenges, including failed negotiations, fractured or distant relationships, and client-service stagnation.

Asking for more in negotiation involves asking the right questions—both of yourself and someone else. What are the questions that hold us back, and which ones help us pave the way forward?

Fishing with a Net: The Power of Open Questions

It's true that most people in negotiation don't ask enough questions. But even when they do, their questions tend to move them further away, not closer to their goal.

I became interested in studying questions early on in my career as a professor and mediator. In the second year of my tenure at Columbia Law School, I was invited to teach in a seaside city in Brazil called Fortaleza. One morning during that trip, prior to one of my mediation lectures at the university, I left my hotel room around sunrise for a walk on nearby Mucuripe Beach.

On the beach I saw the traditional fishing boats called *jangadas*, or rafts, pulling up to the shore, heavy with their stores. Fishermen spread nets on the sand to reveal a rainbow of catch for sale: bacalhau, tuna, shrimp, even pancake stingrays.

Standing on the beach, I thought of my grandmother's waterfront house in Copiague, New York, where as kids we would stand on the dock for hours, holding a fishing line in the bay waters, in hopes of catching one fish to toss back.

With a sudden thought, I rushed back to my hotel room to revise the slides for my lecture.

Standing on the beach in Fortaleza that morning, I realized one of the reasons people tend to feel so stuck when asking questions is because, when we ask questions, we are fishing with a line rather than with a net—meaning, we are asking closed questions that give us very little and often unhelpful information.

Closed questions sound like:

Can I convince this client to upgrade his package with my company?
Should I go back to work full-time and commute, or continue to stay home and feel unfulfilled?
Don't you understand we need to save money this year?
Will my boss give me a $10,000 raise to my base salary?

So how can you tell when you're asking a closed question? Let me give you an example. Imagine asking me about my most recent business trip—let's say to India. What would you ask me?

When I conduct this interview exercise in negotiation workshops, most people tend to ask questions like, "Did you like India?" "What city were you in?" "Was the food spicy?" Those seem like open questions, right? Wrong. Each one of those is a closed question, meaning it invites a yes/no or one-word answer. Every time you ask a closed question, you're fishing with a line.

Want to know an easy way to avoid asking many closed questions? Here it is:

Don't ask a question that starts with a non-action verb (like variations on "be" and "do"). "Was India hot?" "Did the training go well?" "Were you jet-lagged?" "Should I get a guide for the Taj Mahal?" Most of the time, when you start a question with a verb, you are asking a closed question.

Often, we don't realize we are doing this. When you're talking with your best friend and ask a closed question like "Did you like India?," your friend might share more than your question requires. "Yes, I loved India! One of the most interesting things was . . ." But if you're talking to an acquaintance, or someone with whom you're having a conflict? You're likely to get a simple *yes*.

Now that you know this information, you're going to be shocked at the number of closed questions you are asking in your everyday life, both of yourself and others. When you ask closed questions, you are fishing with a line. At most, you will end up with one fish—at worst, you'll leave empty-handed.

What Is an Open Question?

A truly open question is one that invites a broad answer about a number of topics. It prompts the speaker to give you factual information, insight into her feelings, details about her activities, and greater understanding of how she sees herself. As I told my students that first day in Fortaleza, fishing with a net gets you a host of information both good and challenging. You might recover a ton of live fish, as well as some carcasses, or a bunch of kelp that weighs down your net. But you're light-years ahead of the person with one line in the water.

You might be interested to know that this distinction between "open" and "closed" applies beyond the field of negotiation. Lizzie Assa, an expert on childhood play, shared with me that even children's toys can be open-ended or close-ended. What's the difference? With open-ended toys, like a block set of different basic shapes, children (or adults) can build anything. One day it could be a wall to climb, the next day a tree, and the following day a village of people. Open-ended toys promote language, social connection with others, and creativity. (Sound familiar?) Whereas a block set that becomes a firehouse means you can build only one thing: the firehouse. Close-ended toys are better for children who are learning how to pay attention and follow a task to completion.

Likewise, if all we want is to finish a simple task, and do it quickly, a closed question will do the trick. But if we want to solve a challenging problem, see it better, connect better with others and unleash our creativity, we need an open question.

Back to India: The Most Open Question There Is (Hint: It Doesn't Have a Question Mark)

So, you're probably wondering: What's the most open question you can ask about my trip to India? The answer is tricky, because this question doesn't even have a question mark on the end. Here it is: *Tell me about your trip to India!*

This question casts a very wide net. In answering this question, I might tell you that this was my first time in India. That I felt nervous to go because I was recovering from extensive foot surgery and still had a limp. I might tell you how excited I was that our mediation workshop for the Delhi High Court had attracted such a large and engaged

audience. How surprised I was at the warm, family-oriented work culture that prompted the chief justice to invite us to a home-cooked meal
with her own mother. I might describe my awe at seeing the Taj Mahal
at sunrise, my pride at my students' outstanding work, my guilt that my
young daughter was missing me, or my love for onion kulcha. And I
might tell you how optimistic I was that I'd go back. "Tell me" is a magic
question that opens up an entire world to your view. You'll find it later
in this book.

Ten Open Questions: The *Ask for More* Framework

Ask for More contains ten questions that have the power to transform almost any negotiation, business issue, or relationship conflict. In this book,
you'll learn how to ask these ten questions in a way that will change the
way you negotiate, make deals, maintain relationships, and pursue your
dreams.

These will not be safe questions—the closed questions we amateur
fishermen are used to when we leave the house with a pole and a bucket.
Instead, we will ask courageous questions. Open questions. Questions
that will uncover a depth of hidden treasure you never expected.

The Mirror: Getting Clear on Yourself

When people study negotiation, they tend to immediately focus on what
happens when you sit down with (or call, or email) the other side. Should
you make the first offer? Should you assess their strategy and then decide
on yours? How do you frame your demand?

Starting a study of negotiation by talking about the moment you sit
down with someone feels like starting my grandma's tomato sauce recipe
from the moment it hits the pasta. You've missed most of what makes
it work! Any negotiation, any steering conversation, has to begin with
you. You need to steer from the very beginning, by asking yourself the

right questions before you sit down with anyone else. The best nego-tiations, relationships, or client interactions start with you—a process of self-discovery that helps you get clarity on who you are and what you want to achieve.

The first five questions in this book are ones to ask yourself. These open questions will first help you cast a broad net into the deepest re-cesses of your brain and hold up a mirror to yourself. Self-knowledge is critical to making deals and resolving conflict, while also discovering your purpose and finding happiness in life. These questions will help you get there.

Very often what initially brings people into my mediation office is not what they are most concerned with, deep down. They've never been able to ask themselves the questions that perhaps go beyond the money in dispute, the last argument they had with a spouse, or the four corners of the contract that brought them into the room. When I ask them these questions, we unearth what's really driving these disputes—and every-thing makes a lot more sense, including what we're looking for in the upcoming negotiation. This is what I call the "Mirror."

The Window: Getting Clear on Others

After the Mirror questions are five questions to ask someone else in a negotiation. You will use these questions to unlock your window to the person across from you.

Just as you used the Mirror questions to gain perspective on yourself, the Window questions will help you gain perspective on someone else. Never have we needed this ability more than now. Studies of the political and social climate in the United States show that we are more polarized than ever before. Research also demonstrates that people entering the workforce lack sufficient conflict-resolution skills. We can't have the deep conversations that help us steer our families, companies, and society for-ward unless we engage people beyond our own vantage point. We need to have the courage—and the tools—to talk to one another.

Nikhil Seth made the same observation to me about the United Nations:

"It is easy to talk to people who are like-minded. We talk to ourselves much more than crossing the aisle. What really works in negotiation is when you have the courage to take that walk—to go and try and understand another person's or group's perspective. But you have to take that step."

In the process of asking these questions and listening to the answers, I will help you see the other person as clearly as you now see yourself. You will have an unvarnished view of your partner, your boss, your adversary—what makes them tick, what they believe, feel, and need. This kind of perspective is rare and has the power to unlock deals, strengthen relationships, and transform even the most challenging conflicts. That's the "Window."

Bring It Home: Concluding Your Negotiation

By the end of this book, you will have changed the questions you are asking yourself and others. By asking better questions, you get better answers. These questions will expand your view of the world and your place in it. They will expand your view of the people around you. And they will prepare you to approach situations with a more positive, realistic, creative mind-set that will launch you into your next chapter and beyond.

But the journey doesn't end with the questions themselves. Like the Carl Sagan quote at the beginning of this book suggests, asking courageous questions is the start of making our world significant, but it's not the end. We make our world significant—whatever that word means to you—by the depth of our answers.

PART 1

THE MIRROR

Asking Ourselves the Right Questions

You know the feeling. A potential client calls and says, "I'd like to retain you. What's your fee?" Your partner or roommate fires off a text asking why a bill wasn't paid. A recruiter asks you your desired salary. Your tween shows you a teacher's note saying the homework wasn't done again. The real estate agent emails and tells you it's time to make an offer.

And you want to pick up your phone, keyboard—or voice—and respond *right away*.

But hold it. In the Mirror section of this book, you'll learn that by taking a short time—less than thirty minutes—to ask yourself (and answer) five good questions, you'll get much better results, and feel more confident when negotiating with someone else.

In an outward-oriented world in which so much of what we do is performative or focused on others, asking ourselves questions can feel unnatural. Many of us, across professions, have been taught that negotiation competence and leadership is about talking. Or even more than just about talking—that negotiation success means having all the answers.

What does asking ourselves questions have to do with negotiation and steering relationships effectively? Quite a bit, as it turns out. Recent research from organizational psychologist Dr. Tasha Eurich finds a decided link between self-awareness and effective leadership, including negotiation proficiency. But not all self-awareness is created equal. There actually are *two* different kinds of self-awareness: internal and external. Internal self-awareness is our ability to go deep within ourselves and truly see ourselves for who we are: our priorities, needs, emotions, goals, strengths, and weaknesses. External self-awareness is our ability to examine how *others* might see us. Guess which one many of us prioritize? When we focus on how others see us to the detriment of actually understanding ourselves—in other words, when we have high external self-awareness but low internal self-awareness—we are more likely to make choices that don't line up with our values and priorities.

Further, when Dr. Eurich and her team of researchers worked on discovering how to increase self-awareness, guess what they found? That accurate introspection depends on our asking ourselves questions—but not just any questions. In fact, they found that most of us ask ourselves exactly the *wrong* questions.

One of the most ineffective questions people ask when trying to gain perspective on themselves is *why*. For example: "Why did that negotiation go so poorly?" "Why couldn't I land any of my arguments?" *Why* is a question we tend to use when assigning blame, either to others or ourselves. Research shows that asking ourselves *why* puts us in a self-justifying mood and leads to distorted, self-serving answers. It's so pervasive that I've seen it everywhere, often with potentially destructive results. In the days following the 2017 Las Vegas mass shooting, when more than fifty people were killed by a man firing assault rifles from a suite in the Mandalay Bay Hotel, I picked up the *New York Times* and read a piece alleging that in the wake of this tragedy, *why* was the question hanging heaviest over our country.

But in challenging times, *why* isn't the question we most need to ask.

Why looks backward, often seeking to particularize a problem to a perpetrator. But the even bigger problem with *why* is that it's a distancer.

When we feel we understand *why* someone did something, we can blame that *why* and understand how we are separate from it.

You won't find a *why* question in this book, and I don't use *why* questions in negotiation, either. When we ask *why* of ourselves or others, we get self-serving, inaccurate answers. Instead I prefer to ask questions starting with *what*. For example, instead of asking, "Why did I do that?" I might ask, "What went into that decision for me?" Negotiators who ask themselves *what* questions obtain higher levels of internal self-awareness that leads to better business and relationship outcomes.

That most of us lack proficiency in asking ourselves questions makes sense. We have so little practice with talking to ourselves that when we do, we often don't know the right questions to ask. Janet, a human resources executive, told me a story that illustrates this point. She was working with a senior manager, Deborah, who was very unhappy with an employee who'd recently transferred into her group. Deborah vented to Janet that this employee didn't know how she liked things done and she didn't have the time to train someone. She told Janet she needed someone else. She needed someone great.

Janet asked Deborah, "What would a great employee look like?" and gave Deborah space to consider the question. Deborah thought for a minute and said, "Someone who is a good writer, poised and confident, someone with good attention to detail, a great attitude and judgment. Because those are things I can't always teach . . ." And then Deborah's voice trailed off. She paused again, and her eyes opened up. She looked at Janet. "Okay. I got it just now. He does have what I want. I just have to be patient and teach him the ropes." Janet told me, "The magic of this question was that I didn't have to say anything more. Deborah actually called later and said I was a genius because her new employee is such a quick learner!"

As a result of that one Mirror question (*see* chapter 2), Deborah heard her own words and learned something powerful that changed her entire view of the situation—and the situation itself: she had a great employee who needed a bit of investment. After that exchange, Deborah spent some time teaching him the ropes, and her entire team took off in a positive direction.

Your Turn in the Mirror

In the following five chapters, you will ask yourself five great questions that will help you in *any* negotiation. That work starts now. And I have prepared five simple tips to help you.

TIP ONE: CREATE THE OCCASION. Oftentimes, the value I bring as a mediator is that I create the occasion for people in negotiation to tune out the noise and tune in to their issue. I provide a quiet, neutral space in which they can focus. I make them comfortable with drinks and snacks. And I give them as long as they need to talk things through. Do the same for yourself! Block time off. Make it a commitment as firm as a doctor's appointment or a meeting with your boss.

TIP TWO: WRITE DOWN YOUR ANSWERS. Most of us, if we go into an important meeting where we need to listen to someone else's ideas, bring some kind of notepad or device to write things down. Taking notes is not just a sign of respect; it's been proven to help us remember things better. So why don't we do this when we are listening to ourselves? Maybe you're more mindful or organized than I am, but if I don't write something down, I have a hard time remembering it the next day. Research also shows that writing down your goals means you're more likely to achieve them—and that's what you're here to do. So treat this Mirror session like a meeting with yourself. Write down your answers to the questions as the thoughts arise.

TIP THREE: WRITE DOWN THE THING YOU'RE THINKING. Not What You *Wish* You Were Thinking. As you're writing out your answers, you might find yourself cringing as they hit the page. Or worse, you might censor yourself from ever writing them down at all. We are such a judgmental society—and we judge no one quite as harshly and relentlessly as we do ourselves. I can't count the number of times someone has said to me, "Well, this probably wouldn't work, but . . ." or "This is kind of a ridiculous point . . ." before saying something profound and useful. We have an extremely hard time separating ourselves from our internal critic.

But I'm going to ask you to fight against your own judgment in this section. This is important work, for a couple of reasons: First, when we judge ourselves too harshly, we can't see ourselves accurately. In my mediation work, I find one of the most common sources of disputes is people not seeing and presenting themselves as they are. It's one thing to Facetune your online photos so that you look thinner or more awake—but trying to show up in conversation as some idealized, "conflict-tuned" version of yourself always leads to more problems. What happens, for example, when you're *feeling* angry with someone but don't want to acknowledge that to yourself? When you do sit down with the other person, the unfiltered you pops out from behind the curtain, leading to mixed messages, passive aggression, or harsh words you wish later you could take back. Seeing yourself clearly leads to better self-awareness, which in turn helps you to communicate much more clearly and accurately. Others, in turn, will respond to this authenticity—they'll be more likely to share their true selves *and* react positively to your ideas.

TIP FOUR: FOLLOW UP. In this Mirror section, I'm going to give you five great questions that will help you get to know yourself better than ever before. But we won't stop there. I will also help you follow up each question to better understand the things you're hearing about yourself. The follow-up doesn't have to be complicated to be effective. Oftentimes I get the best information from parties after they have answered the first question you'll see in this section, with one simple additional question. After they speak, I thank them, and then ask, "What else would you like us to know?" I can't count the number of times that I *then* hear the thing that has been most on their minds, the thing they were waiting for permission to say. Give yourself that same space and permission.

TIP FIVE: SUMMARIZE YOUR ANSWER. Read your words when you've finished answering each question. Then take a moment and think about what you've uncovered. How would you summarize this answer in a few lines if someone else had said it to you? Tell your story out loud as though you were explaining it to a trusted friend. (Or, if it works better, find an actual friend.) Then write your summary down below your original answer. When you summarize, make sure to look for patterns or words that seem to come up over and over again. Those have special meaning, so take note of them.

Let's get started.

ONE

WHAT'S THE PROBLEM
I WANT TO SOLVE?

Albert Einstein reportedly said that if he had an hour to solve a problem, he would spend fifty-five minutes thinking about the problem and five minutes thinking about solutions.

Another person who loved thinking about problems? Steve Jobs. In 2002, fresh off the success of the iPod, Steve Jobs watched as consumers took to it and used it wherever they went, listening to music. But as he watched (and experienced) this phenomenon, he became less and less satisfied with having created a device that simply added to the weight consumers had to lug around as they traveled. Those same consumers were also burdened with a bunch of other devices: their phone, a bulky laptop, and perhaps even a "personal digital assistant," or PDA, like the Palm. At the time, smartphones and PDAs came with a permanent keyboard that could be difficult for consumers to use, or an attached stylus that sometimes didn't work and was easy to lose.

Jobs saw what others did not: people needed one easy-to-use device for everything, including calls, computing, music, and organization. No keyboard, no stylus or other writing tool that could be lost. Just one device and the only accessory it needed: the human finger. He set Apple's engineers to work on creating the *one* device that would solve this problem.

Several years later, Jobs walked out of a meeting with AT&T, having negotiated a deal for their subsidiary Cingular Wireless to carry the first ever iPhone—which, remarkably, was still in development. AT&T would have exclusive distribution rights to the new iPhone, and in return, Apple would get approximately ten dollars from each customer's wireless bill every month. Apple also retained control over the phone's software, pricing, distribution, and branding. This type of deal had never been seen before in the wireless phone industry. Jobs brought AT&T on board by describing a problem he believed only Apple could solve, and articulating his vision for a groundbreaking solution.

This negotiation was only part of a larger series of negotiations by Jobs to bring the iPhone to life. A consultant who worked with Jobs at the time, Raj Aggarwal, told *Forbes* magazine that the success of this one negotiation with AT&T resulted, in part, from the way Jobs steered his relationships with all the relevant players: "Jobs met with the CEOs of each carrier. I was struck by his hands-on nature and his desire to make his mark on everything the company was doing." He steered every detail of the product with his engineers, testing and testing until the product worked the way he envisioned. He steered his relationships with consultants like Aggarwal, with his colleagues at Apple, with analysts in the market—and, most important, with his customers.

The Apple iPhone, released in 2007, quickly captured a sizable segment of the mobile market. What led to this transformative success for Jobs and Apple? As Kevin Ashton, a British technology entrepreneur who profiled Jobs, later described: "For Jobs and the iPhone, the critical point of departure was not finding a solution but seeing a problem: the problem of permanent keyboards making smarter phones harder to use. Everything else followed."

The First Critical Step in *Any* Negotiation

The first question to ask yourself in any negotiation is "What's the problem I want to solve?"

Remember, to negotiate is to steer. Every decision, every turn you make in a negotiation stems from the problem or goal you have defined for yourself. In other words, if you're going to be paddling your kayak, don't you first want to know where you're going? People who skip this step (and many do) run the risk of finding themselves having paddled all day through choppy waters, only to find themselves on the wrong island.

Most people think that the fun part of negotiation is figuring out the solution. Nope. This—defining your problem—is the juicy work. Once you learn how to define a problem, you'll find how incredibly satisfying, creative, and even fun it can be. For me as a negotiation coach, helping you find your *what*, your problem to solve, feels just as exhilarating as some people find jumping out of a plane or eating an incredibly fresh plate of pasta in Italy. (Don't judge; we all like different things.) And that's because I know what incredible things you might find or achieve on the other side of this question.

Defining the problem helps you create the solution. And that's the case for any negotiation, whether you're facing a large diplomatic conflict or just trying to convince your toddler that ice cream is not dinner.

Spending Time to Save Time

It takes a bit of time to accurately define your problem. But usually, the time you spend at the beginning comes back to you. One executive who took my negotiation course and completed this question told me, "I think in the space of fifteen minutes I have probably saved myself three days of spinning my wheels." When you know where you want to steer, you save a lot of time that otherwise might be spent checking your map and doubling back.

Defining the Problem in Big Negotiations

Defining your problem is critically important for big, long-standing, or complicated negotiations. Put another way: if someone came to my office and I were to immediately ask about the solution to their problem, I'd be asking them to describe something they can't even see. Imagine that you are hiking up a mountain. The taller the mountain, the less you can see the top from where you stand at the base. You need to start at the bottom, working your way up step-by-step. With each rocky path you traverse, or stream you ford, you gain experience and confidence that helps you continue. And at some point, the summit becomes visible. You're able to picture what it looks like and how you will get there.

As we hike up a mountain, so too do we negotiate. By asking yourself what problem you want to solve, you are starting where you need to start—with the problem you're trying to solve—and generating information that will help you visualize and reach your goal, which is your solution.

Let's take an example. One big problem the United States faces is the chronic absence of some children from school. Chronic absence, defined as missing 10 percent or more of school days due to absence for any reason, can translate into third graders unable to master reading, sixth graders failing subjects, and ninth graders dropping out of high school. According to non-profit Attendance Works, which helps schools and community partners work together to reduce chronic absence, every year more than eight million students in the United States miss so many days of school that they become academically at risk in the ways described above.

Traditionally, people looking at the problem of chronic absence tended to focus only on what was called "truancy," or unexcused absence from school—meaning days when students did not have a parental note excusing them from class. This one-sided definition of the problem assumed inappropriate student or family behavior, and often led to a knee-jerk, punitive solution: penalties for both students and parents in an effort to force better behavior. But the penalties didn't work.

When Hedy Chang, executive director of Attendance Works, sat down to define the problem, she didn't focus on unexcused absences and suspensions. Instead, she defined the problem as kids missing significant amounts of school for any reason. Indeed, in the early grades, she found that many at-risk students were accumulating excused absences, meaning that focusing on truancy wouldn't catch the problem.

With that problem definition guiding her, Hedy encourages schools to uncover the actual problems preventing kids from attending school by talking with kids and parents. These efforts have led to unexpected solutions. Once they opened lines of communication with their students and families, principals at a number of schools found something unexpected: sometimes, kids skipped school not to avoid the work, or because their parents didn't prioritize learning, but because their clothes weren't clean. Students who didn't have a way to clean their clothes would stay home rather than feel embarrassed in front of their peers. Armed with this discovery, a growing number of schools partnered with local businesses or foundations to provide clothes-washing services at school. One school reported that the percentage of students attending school 90 percent of the time jumped from 46 percent to 84 percent after combining the clothes-washing program with check-ins from caring mentors. Broadly defining the problem of chronic absence helped Hedy, Attendance Works, educators and community partners from around the country design one innovative, effective solution that benefited families and districts alike.

As this example shows, if you're dealing with a big or complicated negotiation, it's critical to define your problem. This is true of personal situations, too. Take Antonia, a financially successful insurance professional who, for the last five years, has been in conflict with her older sister, Carmen. Carmen repeatedly asks Antonia for financial help and then spends the money not on housing or food, but on luxury items that she can show off to her friends. To make things worse, Carmen speaks disdainfully about Antonia's career success to the rest of their family. Antonia feels more and more resentful, and yet every time she tries to talk to Carmen, she has trouble articulating anything beyond her anger. The conversations never seem to move the situation forward, or give Antonia any relief. The reason? Antonia needs to define the problem she wants to solve. Is it asking Carmen to show appreciation for Antonia's help? Setting boundaries around money? Finding a way to tactfully take a break from the relationship? Knowing the problem she wants to solve will give her a roadmap for the conversation she needs to have.

Ever sit down with someone and find yourself having trouble organizing information or prioritizing what means the most to you? Or maybe you're ten years into your career and throwing yourself into a variety of initiatives, but at the end of the day you're not sure what you're progressing toward? Like Antonia, you may have skipped the important step in which you define your problem.

Defining the Problem in Simple Negotiations

Maybe you're not trying to cure cancer or even determine the course of your career. You're just preparing to talk to your contractor about what you're doing with your bathroom, or trying to get your landlord's attention to fix a leak. Seems like you should just be able to start talking solutions, yes?

Let's take the bathroom example. You're preparing to sit down with your contractor to go over a prospective renovation. Even here, it makes sense to ask what the problem is that you're trying to solve. Are you selling your house? If so, maybe you're trying to design a commercially appealing bathroom at a reasonable cost. Are you settling into your dream home, where if all goes well, you will be spending the next four decades of your life? If so, you might be trying to include all the cutting-edge features you will want to use during that time. Or are you redoing the bathroom in a hurry because your partner had an accident and is now confined to a wheelchair? If so, you have a whole other set of choices to consider.

Even in simple negotiations, you can't design solutions until you understand the problem.

Defining a Problem No One Else Has Seen Yet: Innovation as Negotiation

Sometimes in negotiation we are steering our kayak by "picking a line" through the rapids carved out by the person in front of us. And sometimes, there's no line to pick; we have to create it.

I started this chapter with a story about innovation that is also a negotiation story. How? Apple figured out where it needed to go and steered its important relationships—with its distributor, the market, and its customers—in that direction. And it all started with defining the problem.

Most people think negotiation is mostly backward-looking, but negotiation is steering. It is creative. It is generative. Ultimately, negotiation is how we create our future. Sometimes we do that by solving a problem before anyone else even comprehends it. That creative place is where negotiation becomes innovation.

Steve Jobs recognized this. Jobs always sought to understand the next problem (recognizing that there is always a problem, even with products that consumers apparently love) and solve it—sometimes before anyone else in the market even recognized there was a problem. On Apple's campus there is an inscription that reads INFINITE LOOP. What does that mean? It means that, as author Kevin Ashton described in studying Jobs, "Creating is not a result of genius, unconscious incubation, or aha! moments. It is a result of thinking: a series of mental steps consisting of problem, solution, repeat."

Darrell Mann, a global innovation expert who formerly served as the chief engineer at Rolls-Royce, has spent decades studying innovation efforts by companies, and what makes them work—or not. He found that only 2 percent of companies' innovation efforts succeeded. And of those, "Twenty-five percent of failures were due to people trying to solve the wrong problems."

How to Define Your Problem Completely: Getting the "Bigger Picture" Perspective

"What's the problem I want to solve?" is a broad question, one we often need to challenge ourselves to answer accurately. Neuroscience research from *Thinking, Fast and Slow* and similar works tells us that humans tend to avoid challenging questions in favor of answering narrower, easier questions instead. We do this to avoid dealing with things we're not sure how to answer or which we'd rather not confront. But fishing with a net when solving a problem can lead to tremendous discoveries that change everything.

Marcus, the head of a regional office for a nationwide company, sat down with his managers to solve a problem. An employee, Roger, had sought a promotion and been denied, causing him to make an internal complaint. When his managers initially called this meeting, they had decided the problem they wanted to solve was settling Roger's complaint without going to court. But they ended up diagnosing a much larger problem.

In thinking about Roger's claim, Marcus was confused about what was happening in this one city office under his jurisdiction. This used to be a happy team that appeared tight-knit. But in the last year, three employees had filed complaints that they were being treated unfairly, whether on work assignments, overtime, or with manager communication. Nothing about management had changed. Work assignments seemed to have been distributed as usual.

Marcus put Roger's complaint to the side for a minute; instead, he zoomed out and asked his team to talk more broadly about how things were going in the office this year. His managers discussed current personnel numbers, the kinds of work they were tackling, and the status of their building reorganization—and that's where things got interesting for Marcus. He remembered that in the last year, that office had been going through a space renovation and reorganization. Because of the construction, they had to relocate a third of their employees away from the others into a much older space. Marcus asked where Roger and the other two employees with complaints currently sat. All of them had been relocated.

Marcus realized that his problem was not "How can we settle Roger's complaint without going to court?" Instead, it was "How can we return our office to a cohesive and well-functioning unit?" Marcus spoke to Roger directly, and instead of just talking about the promotion, he asked Roger to talk more generally about life around the office. Roger had, in fact, felt shut out of office decisions recently. No one had told him why he was part of the group that had been moved. Communication among his team had suffered. Before, when they all worked in the same space, Roger used to be able to drop by his supervisors' offices regularly, but that didn't happen anymore. Even worse, no one had talked to Roger after the promotion decisions came down. Instead, he heard about them via email.

Understanding this larger problem proved key to helping Marcus settle Roger's promotion complaint and much more. Marcus and the management team met with all the employees in the office and took responsibility for not communicating effectively about the office and space decisions they had made. They brought the employees into the discussion about what was happening with the renovations. They engaged the entire office in finding ways to improve communication with employees across the two spaces. Marcus successfully resolved all three employee complaints and got the office back on track. Understanding a larger view of the problem posed by Roger's case helped Marcus craft a negotiation strategy that worked not just for Roger but for the entire office.

The goal of this chapter is to get you started on actually solving your problem, so you will need to take the time to cast a wide net in order to get the broadest possible view. This is what innovation experts call getting the "bigger picture" perspective. Once you've defined your problem, you will learn how to zoom out from it and see if there is a bigger picture you're missing.

What Not to Do: The Usual Ways We Define a Problem

Many of us skip the critical negotiation step in which we define our problem. And I've seen people settle for less in negotiation because they defined their problem in a limited, unhelpful way. Let me give you an example:

Rosana, a CEO, has just received employee survey results from her head of Human Resources. Seeing higher than usual turnover among her more junior employees, she asked HR to survey them and ask about their satisfaction at work. The survey results indicate that morale among junior employees is quite low. Imagine that Rosana sits down to define her problem to solve, and writes:

Our junior employee satisfaction rating is extremely low.

Any problem with this definition? Several, actually. First, it looks backward. Yes, we want to focus on the problem before jumping into designing solutions, but we also need to define our problem in a way that gives us a clear destination to steer toward. Nothing about this problem definition helps Rosana think about the future of her business. Second, it's framed in the negative. It focuses on where she doesn't want to be instead of where she does. We don't want to get in the kayak, and when someone asks us where we are going, say, "Well, I know I *don't* want to end up on the rocks." Last, talking about the *rating* is a pretty narrow way to define the problem, like fishing with a line. Likely the rating is merely symbolic of a much larger issue Rosana will need to solve.

Five Steps to Defining Your Problem Clearly and Completely

For the first step, take five minutes to consider and write down the problem *you* want to solve, whether that's a major family challenge like Antonia's, working with a contractor on your bathroom renovation, or trying to restore morale in your office. Include any issues you think may have contributed to the situation as it stands today, as well as the effects these issues are having on your life, career, company, or community. For example, Rosana might complete this section by talking about employee turnover, the survey, the results, and anything else that comes to mind as a part of this problem. Next, once you're finished writing, I want you to take what you've written and summarize it in one sentence, as Rosana did above. Summarizing your problem in one sentence helps to give you the clearest, most concise picture possible. Rosana did this when she wrote, "Our junior employee satisfaction rating is extremely low." For our bathroom contractor example, this could look like, "The total quote came in too high for my budget." And for Antonia, that sentence may be "My sister disrespects me and doesn't thank me for anything I've done."

Third, take anything that is negative and backward-looking in that sentence and reframe it to be positive and forward-looking. When we define a problem to solve, we need to spell out what we want in the future, not what we didn't want in the past. For example, Rosana would change "Our junior employee satisfaction rating is extremely low" to "We need to achieve high junior employee satisfaction levels." Our homeowner might move from "The total quote was too high" to "I need a bathroom that will work for my budget." And Antonia would change "My sister disrespects me and doesn't thank me for anything I've done" to "I need respect and acknowledgment from my sister." When you're steering your kayak, you achieve better results when you're focused on the goal (the beach) instead of the obstacle (the rocks). By making this shift, we move from a place of fear or complaint to a positive problem-solving mind-set that carries us to our destination.

Fourth, take your sentence and change it into a question starting with *how*, *what*, *who*, or *when*. Rosana would do this by asking, "What can we do to achieve high junior employee satisfaction levels?" or "How can we achieve high levels of junior employee satisfaction?" Our homeowner might ask, "How can I get a new bathroom that will work for my budget?"

And Antonia would ask, "How can I feel respected and acknowledged by my sister?" A similar message, but phrased as a question, motivates you to seek more concrete information and to act on it. Yet again, questions are the answer when it comes to negotiation.

Last, we want to define your problem broadly and capture the full picture. If your initial problem definition was narrow, like Rosana's, there's a good reason why. Your brain is working against you, wanting to fish with a line instead of a net. Look at the question you just wrote and ask yourself, "What would happen if this came true?" Then write that answer down and consider revising your original question to reflect a larger picture. Here, Rosana would look at her question, "What can we do to achieve high junior employee satisfaction levels?" and ask herself, "What would happen if junior employee satisfaction rose?" She might conclude that with higher satisfaction levels, her company would attract and retain the best employees, and achieve even better results. Rosana's revised question would then read: "What can we do to make this company a place where the best people in the industry want to apply, stay, and work their hardest toward our increased success?" In this way, Rosana has turned a conversation about the survey rating into a call to action that will help her steer her company and all those relationships forward. Our homeowner might look at her question and figure out that if she achieved a better budgetary result on her bathroom, she might be able to contribute more money to her 401K this year. So the revised question could be, "How can I achieve a budget on this bathroom that will allow me to save more toward retirement?" And Antonia might change, "How can I feel respected and acknowledged by my sister?" to "How can I achieve a relationship with my sister that feels emotionally healthy enough to sustain?" This question clarifies for Antonia that this isn't just about money, or a disrespectful interaction; it's evaluating what she needs in order to continue a relationship with Carmen.

As the examples above show, too often we define our problems reactively, based on just one interaction or situation. Each of these revised questions allows for the person involved to move beyond an immediate triggering event—a survey, an outdated bathroom, a fight with a sibling— to consider the broader goals they're seeking: a successful company, a robust retirement fund, or overall emotional health. That's the bigger picture you need to define in order to *ask for more* in negotiation.

Troubleshooting Common Questions

Here are a couple of common questions I get when discussing "What's the problem I want to solve?"

What about the Problems That Can't Be Solved?

Even conflict resolution experts recognize that some problems have no solution. Sometimes, the best we can do is simply *manage*. For example, as I write this book, I am working through what feels like an impossible set of choices about how best to care for my dying father. He needs twenty-four-hour assistance, and we must decide whether to place him in a skilled nursing unit where he will be safe but will miss his family greatly, or keep him at home, where he might hurt himself, and where my stepmother and his health aides are suffering stress. There is no perfect, or even happy, solution here. No negotiation strategies can change the fact that my father has an incurable, degenerative brain disease, and that he will continue to suffer in any living situation as the disease progresses. And yet, I'm still working through these questions to help me as we make these decisions. Even for problems that are unsolvable, understanding the problem helps us minimize the damaging effects it has on our lives, decrease the stress and anxiety we feel as a result of it, and may even help us discover new strategies.

And even if you can't solve the underlying problem ("How can we cure frontotemporal dementia?" left me nowhere), you can still find something to address. I worked through this question when making medical decisions for my dad, and my final problem definition turned out to be: "How can we care for Dad in a way that maximizes his comfort and dignity and also allows his family caregivers to feel supported?" Seeing the problem this way, and working through the rest of the questions in this section, made the decision clear: we transferred him to a memory care facility where he could receive expert treatment and also daily visits from family. We can't cure my dad's illness, but we can prioritize his comfort and dignity, as well as the family's well-being. Often, having an achievable goal in the midst of an unsolvable problem can bring a sense of peace.

What If I'm Only Negotiating with Myself?

We know that negotiation also means steering the conversation you have with yourself. Should I speak up in management meetings? Is it time for me to go into business as an entrepreneur? How can I feel more confident when I advocate for myself in my personal relationships? This question, and the Mirror section of this book, can be very useful in any of these negotiations.

Sometimes, people seek out negotiation coaching not because they're ready to sit down with someone else, but because they're feeling stuck and need clarity on a decision. That stuck feeling is usually an internal negotiation. What am I meant to do with my life? Which job should I take? Should I go back to work? How can I feel happier? Many people believe that it takes two to make a conflict, but you only need one car to have an accident!

When you examine what brought you to this place, you'll have better information to help you move through it. If you're internally stuck, you can still go through both sides of the situation and look at the conflicting feelings, patterns, and facts that are leading to the stagnation you feel.

Self-Censoring: Too Many Cooks in Your Mental Kitchen

One of the main problems I deal with in mediation or negotiation counseling is helping people combat their self-censorship and define their own goals for themselves. You might feel like your goal should be X, but really you're yearning for Y.

I once had a student come to my office. He was one of the strongest performers in my class, and indeed had succeeded similarly in other classes. With a top academic record, he set a goal of getting into the best firm he could. (In this context, "best" means "highest ranked." Lawyers love rankings.) In law school, students spend the summer interning at the law firm they hope to work for after graduation. If they nab a permanent job offer, they get to return for their last year at law school knowing they are set. This student, whom I'll call David, succeeded in getting job offers at many of the best law firms in the country, and went to the top firm on his list for a summer internship. After spending a summer in their offices, the firm enthusiastically offered him a permanent job.

David returned to school in September and asked me for a meeting. He arrived at my office, shut the door and looked around, as though worried someone might overhear him. In a quiet voice, he told me he'd had a great summer. Then he paused.

"But . . . ?" I asked.

"But . . ." he said, "I don't know. My original goal was just to go to the highest-ranked firm. And it's a great place. I'm lucky to have a job there. If I'm being honest, though, I don't know if that's the life I want for myself. I want a family. I want to spend time with them. And . . . I also play in a band. I really want time to make music."

"Great," I said. "So why do you look like you're apologizing to me?"

"Well," he said, "because I feel like it's not socially acceptable to . . . want a life."

I laughed out loud, and after a moment he joined me. Sometimes, having a life feels like a revolutionary goal. That day, we talked more about this goal and ways he could achieve it, alongside his other career goals. I'm pleased to report that today, this former student works at a place where he has a life. He plays music, and is an active parent to his kids. These were worthy goals, and he's achieved them.

What do you do if someone else's voice is in your head as you're writing answers to this question? You might be getting confused by or preoccupied with what someone else thinks is the problem. Engage with that question: write down the different audiences to your issue—maybe your coworkers, clients, spouse, kids—and ask yourself what their views of the problem would be. Then study that. What seems right to you about what you wrote? What doesn't resonate? Eventually, your goal will be to move that perspective to the side so that you can tune in to your own sense of your problem.

"I Don't Know"

What if you read this question and draw a blank? Maybe you aren't sure what has brought you to the point of reading this book. You might be a negotiation avoider. Some people I know are so good at avoiding negotiation that they manage to forget they need to do it at all. This is the equivalent of not only putting down your kayak paddle but also then sticking your head between your knees and letting the current take you wherever.

Or you might know you need to negotiate, but you're not quite sure where to begin with thinking about your problem. Sometimes when we are in conflict or in the middle of an ongoing situation or challenging negotiation, we're left feeling like everything is a big jumbled mess and we're not sure where to start untangling it.

If you see yourself in either of these paragraphs, try this:

Ask yourself the last few times you felt dissatisfied, restless, unhappy, or fed up. What happened just before those moments? This may help you define the problem you want to solve.

Or try the reverse: ask yourself the last few times you felt happy, satisfied, or like things were on the right track. What happened to produce those moments? This may lead you to discover your goal.

And if you're still drawing a blank: take a break. Instead, I want you to focus on the next few moments in which you're feeling unhappy/happy and notice what preceded that feeling. Now you're getting close to discovering what's brought you to the point of reading this book and taking action. Remember that defining your problem, or your goal, will be the foundation on which you build your solution.

Wrapping Up

Identifying the problem you want to solve is the first vital step to mastering negotiation. Now that you've thoroughly defined the problem, we'll delve into some of what's underlying your issue.

TWO

WHAT DO I NEED?

Lilia looked at the somber faces of her new staff members as they departed her office. It was 2013, and Lilia, a professor, lawyer, and researcher, had recently been promoted to vice president of the University of Fortaleza (UNIFOR), a private university in northeast Brazil. Her position put her in charge of all their graduate programs.

When she took over the vice presidency, Lilia had dreamed about taking UNIFOR's graduate programs to a new level, raising the numbers of students enrolled as well as its national rankings. But that day, Lilia's staff went to her to share their concerns. The overall health of their graduate school programs was poor. With Brazil's economic situation unsteady and unemployment rates above 7 percent, UNIFOR struggled to attract graduate students. UNIFOR was a private graduate school that relied heavily on people to have jobs and the financial means to afford their tuition. Without jobs, people worried about investing in graduate education and spending substantial amounts of money on what they saw as an uncertain return. UNIFOR's peer schools wouldn't release their graduate school numbers, but Lilia's staff heard that they were struggling, too. Her staff warned her to brace for impact, that the picture looked bleak and there seemed little they or anyone could do to change things until the overall economic climate improved. Their definition of the problem could have been summed up as follows: "We won't be able to increase student enrollments, or our rankings, until Brazil is through this economic crisis and more people get jobs."

Lilia saw things differently. She wondered how UNIFOR could use its graduate programs to help people get through the crisis and find employment, thereby offering hope instead of cost. Lilia investigated what UNIFOR needed to solve this problem. She realized that they needed to offer not just an education in the substance of students' chosen fields, like business, law, or urban planning, but management skills that would make them attractive to employers. She also knew that the university would need to find a way to connect people to jobs through the graduate programs themselves. Finally, Lilia thought about what she personally needed: "As a researcher, I was used to identifying problems and solving them. I got a high every time I managed to find an innovative way around something that seemed impossible. And I was also a professional woman who'd had my first child very early, before even finishing my education— so I was used to getting creative and persevering in my personal life, too. I realized that I couldn't give up on the dream of expanding our graduate programs, for me as much as anyone else. It wouldn't just hurt UNIFOR; it would hurt me. I needed this challenge as much as the institution did."

Based on this list of needs, Lilia restructured UNIFOR's graduate programs to offer not only technical skills in each chosen field, but management skills like conflict resolution, complex problem-solving, creativity, and teamwork. She also devised a capstone component to every one of their graduate programs, whereby students were required to create a final project that would link their studies to the outside world in order to solve a problem, whether local or international. UNIFOR would then connect them with a company or government agency that needed that work. Lilia called this new model of graduate education "Leaders Who Transform,"

and communicated directly with the public about how a UNIFOR graduate education could benefit them not despite, but *because* of the difficult
economic climate. Indeed, unemployed students who enrolled in UNI-
FOR's programs started to get jobs as a result of Lilia's efforts to connect
them to practice. The enrollment numbers began to turn around.

In 2019, Lilia sat down again to evaluate UNIFOR's graduate programs. Brazil's economic situation had indeed changed from when she
started "Leaders Who Transform" back in 2013: it was worse. Unemployment had climbed to nearly 13 percent. And yet, the total number of
students enrolled in her graduate programs had *doubled*. Moreover, the
Brazilian agency regulating all graduate programs changed the standards
by which it evaluated the quality of master's programs and PhDs to include the "impact of the research/project on society"—a direct result of
the work they saw being done at UNIFOR.

Reframing the problem, and focusing on her personal and institutional needs, helped Lilia transform the entire graduate division of
UNIFOR, as well as the lives of many people across Brazil.

We Need, Therefore We Do (or Don't)

Needs motivate everything we do. They are our driving forces, the *why*
behind all human behavior. You'll know something is a need for you, as
opposed to just a wish or a want, if the lack of it causes you some kind of
suffering or adversity. Whether or not we think about or are even aware
of our needs in any given moment, they exist—and they influence what
we do or don't do, every minute of our lives.

People often prepare for negotiation by thinking about their "bottom
line," otherwise known as the worst-case scenario that could still result in
a deal. But studies show that those who instead focus on identifying their
goals, also called aspirations, get more from their negotiations—especially
aspirations that are "optimistic, specific, and justifiable." How do we find
those aspirations? By identifying our needs. When we set goals based on
our real needs, we negotiate from a place of clarity and conviction that

helps us aspire to more. We steer more confidently and with more accuracy toward our goal. I am often asked: "How do you know when to walk away from a negotiation?" "How do you stand firm on your goal?" "How do you ask for more, and do it confidently?" My answer to these three questions is the same: you negotiate based on a thorough understanding of your deepest needs. Your needs are your clarity and your strength.

By contrast, when we go into negotiation, or even through life, without understanding our needs, we become rudderless. We are sitting in the kayak with a paddle in our lap, at the mercy of the wind and waves. We may feel scattered, disorganized, panicked. We never find our destination because we don't know which way to steer.

Even though our needs are critical to negotiation, we often don't uncover them without asking ourselves the right questions. In this chapter, you'll learn how to do just that.

Identifying Your Needs

"What do I need?" is an important question. It helps you get to the root of any problem or negotiation. And it takes practice and patience to answer it fully.

Here, you will ask yourself what you need and write down your response. I'm going to guide you through the different types of needs that can come up when people answer this question. And I will propose a couple of very important follow-up questions to ask yourself in order to make those needs concrete and actionable, so you can move forward with confidence toward your aspirations. We'll also examine how to uncover the needs you've been hiding even from yourself, and what to do when you have needs that appear to conflict.

Your Turn in the Mirror

I want you to begin this exercise by giving yourself time to contemplate the question of what you need. I suggest you write down your answers before we delve into the broader topic of human needs in general. Get into a comfortable place, turn off your phone, and devote yourself to looking in the Mirror. Set aside five minutes to write down whatever comes to mind. Remember, no self-censorship! If you think it, even for a fraction of a second, write it down, just as it is. And if you get nothing but silence to start, that's fine. Sit quietly for a few minutes. Give yourself the gift of your patience and time (it's only five minutes) to answer this question: *What do I need?*

If you write a few things and then feel stuck, imagine me asking you, "What else?" or "Can you say more about [what you've just written down]?" Keep going until five minutes are up.

To Have Needs Is Human; to Understand Them, Divine

I deliberately started this chapter with you, because I wanted to give you the freedom to answer this question for yourself before priming you with research on, and more examples of, other people's needs.

So now that you've given this some thought, let's analyze needs more generally. What are they? How do we think about them? How can we make sense of what we need, and what those needs mean for our negotiation?

The Problem: We Confuse Needs with Other Stuff

We have so little practice identifying our own needs that we can get them confused with other things. Needs are different from emotions, for example. If you're feeling a certain way about a situation, generally it's because you have a need that is (or isn't) being met. We feel what we feel because we need what we need.

We also frequently confuse needs with our negotiation demands or positions. For example: "I've waited ten years for a promotion to VP; now it's my turn. I should be the very next one from our division who gets promoted." Or: "I always plan our outings with the kids—I'm not doing it today." And in a legal case, demands are what's contained in the case documents, such as: "He breached our contract, and I'm owed damages of fifty thousand dollars."

The challenge in identifying our needs is that they aren't always explicit. So we focus on our demands, which are easier to identify because they often relate to money or something tangible.

So what's the difference between needs and demands? Needs are the reasons *why* we make demands. When you uncover your needs, you get valuable information that helps you *and* the other person have a more successful negotiation.

Human Needs in Negotiation

Having spent more than a decade mediating conflicts of every kind, I've seen many of the same basic human needs come up over and over again. But needs can also be as varied and diverse as humans themselves. Experts in many disciplines, from anthropology to psychology and law, have thought about and created ways to organize and think about needs.

In this section I will highlight several categories of needs that human beings experience. Drawn from psychology research, they transcend gender, culture, and subject matter. We will talk about basic physical needs first and then move on to social, emotional, and other needs. Let's take a brief look through these categories and see which of them resonates with you.

Basic Biological Needs: First Things First

Our most fundamental needs as human beings are basic physical needs: food, clothing, shelter, sleep, sex, air, and water. For many of us, these needs come first; we must have our basic physical needs met before we can function well enough to turn our attention to any higher-order needs, like financial advancement or emotional satisfaction.

I've seen how "physical needs first" rings true. I have encountered many cases in New York City Civil Court where one of the parties to a dispute is food insecure or homeless. I recall one case in which a landlord was suing a former tenant for back rent. The court asked us to have the parties negotiate. We brought both parties to our mediation room inside the courthouse, where the defendant sat silently on one side of the table, huddled up and shivering—even though the temperature inside the room was quite warm. When it was his turn to speak, he sheepishly asked us for a little time, saying he was having trouble formulating his thoughts. My students, reading the situation, called for a private session (a mediator move in which we talk to each party individually) so that he could talk to us without the pressure of having the other party present. Once we were alone, the former tenant opened up to us. He told us that he was homeless, and that even for some time before that, he had not had enough to eat. He said, "I don't mean to be dramatic or whatever, but I swear . . . it's hard to think when the fridge is empty." I greatly admired this man's efforts to participate in negotiation despite the fact that he was suffering and hungry. We ultimately decided that we could better use our time together to connect him with resources to help meet his basic physical needs. We left him our Mediation Clinic number to call when he was in a better place and ready to negotiate his case.

This relationship between hunger and conflict also exists on the world stage. David Beasley, executive director of the World Food Programme, says, "The link between hunger and conflict is as strong as it is destructive. Conflict leads to food insecurity. And food insecurity can also stoke instability and tension, which trigger violence." Globally, according to Beasley, 60 percent of the 815 million chronically food-insecure people live in conflict areas.

Even if we are not dealing with food insecurity or the effects of war, we all share these basic human needs. Physiological needs are the reason that, when I mediate disputes, I make sure all parties have plenty of food, drinks, and time for breaks. We have a hard time focusing when those physical needs aren't met. Don't neglect food, water, and rest—for you and for others—when you negotiate.

Safety and Security Needs

The next category of needs is safety, which includes security and economic stability. These interests often feel more urgent for human beings than the needs we'll discuss after.

Safety, or the sense of protection from harm, is a fundamental need for all human beings. I once invited diplomats from Kosovo to come to Columbia Law School and talk about the peace process that gave birth to their nation. All of them said that their "freedom" or sovereignty did not begin until Kosovo's citizens, who had been ravaged by famine and violence, were fed and safe; only as the fear subsided could they even begin to think about progress or political stature. If your list of needs includes basics like safety, you may have to focus on this need first, before addressing the secondary needs farther down in this section.

Our human need for security also affects many of our everyday choices and concerns. In the daily decisions we make, some of us are what I call "security negotiators"—meaning that we value certainty and lowering risk over saving money or other needs.

During a negotiation training workshop I held for U.S. government officials, one participant, Mikayla, described a frustrating interaction she had recently had with her husband over day-care arrangements for their son. Their agency was in the process of cutting down on telework, meaning that she and her husband would need to find new care arrangements. She found a beautiful, safe facility close to home that had a spot available. It was on the higher end of their price range, but it fit their needs, and she was ready to close the deal. Balking at the high price tag, he insisted that they try to look around for something a little cheaper. Exasperated, Mikayla discussed the situation with her colleagues.

I said, "It sounds like your need for security is trumping your need to maximize the economics of this situation."

She said, "Yes, actually, that's true! I'm big on security. For me, as long as a big decision is open, I worry. What if the day care fills up? What if nothing else turns out to be better? I'd rather have it settled. When we looked for houses, I was the same way. As soon as we found one that worked, I was done. Having it settled made me feel so relieved."

This official prioritized the security of having a day-care spot secured. Meanwhile, her husband had a higher need for economic efficiency. They negotiated with the day care to give them some time to make a decision. And Mikayla and her husband agreed that if they couldn't mutually settle on another, cheaper day care in that time, they would go with the facility she had found and find another way to save costs in their budget. Setting a timeline allowed Mikayla to feel secure, and gave her husband some assurance that either way, they'd be making efforts on the financial front.

Financial security rounds out the list of these fundamental needs. Money allows us to buy the necessities of life. It means food, health insurance, childcare, and a safety net for emergencies. When people negotiate for their salary or the value of a contract, they may have in mind specific needs that will be fulfilled by that money. If a person's economic needs are pressing, they may value economic stability above anything else, including title or quality of life. But, as you'll see later in this chapter, money also connects to other, less concrete needs.

Psychological and Emotional Needs

Think you can take psychology and emotion out of negotiation? Think again. *All* negotiations, even those that center on finances, involve psychological and emotional needs. These can include:

Love and belonging needs, which include love, acceptance, social support, belonging, intimacy, affection, and affiliation (which is defined as feeling part of a group, whether at work or with friends or at home). That these needs come up in personal negotiations is not surprising. We need few things more than the love and support of those closest to us.

Sometimes people read words like "love," "belonging," and "esteem," and ask me if these needs actually come up in work-centered negotiations. The answer is: all the time. In my experience, people often ask or sue for money because they can't contract for love, appreciation, or acceptance. We spend a lot of our lives at work, and studies show that whether we feel we belong, whether we have friendships and connections there, is a major determinant of both happiness and productivity.

Esteem needs, both self-esteem-focused (dignity, pride, achievement, accomplishment) and those that focus on the esteem of others (like respect, reputation, recognition, or status). One of the things I love about assisting people in their negotiations is seeing the sense of pride and accomplishment radiating off them when they achieve a great result for themselves. In fact, self-esteem needs may be one of the things that drove you to pick up this book. You, too, may want more pride, achievement, and accomplishment from your life. If that's you, stay tuned: later in this chapter, I'll show you how to turn those powerful needs into an action plan that brings you closer to realizing them.

Esteem needs underlie personal negotiations as well as business and diplomatic ones. Four major needs in this category are respect, dignity, recognition, and reputation.

I have never yet seen a negotiation in which respect, which means admiration for someone or consideration for their feelings, rights, or wishes, was not critically important for success. Marriage researcher John Gottman has studied respect for decades and found that lack of respect in a partnership is one of the "Four Horsemen" that predicts divorce. Likewise, in business, research shows that when people receive respect, they are more likely to give it in return. Respect creates trust—and deals.

Dignity, which in some cultures is called "face," is very important for people in all situations. From cradle to grave, every human being craves a sense of pride and worthiness in themselves—and whether that need is met is critical to their well-being, or even their will to live. When my father's hospice agency helped my father make one final trip back to his home to spend time with his family, I was surprised and touched to see that even as he struggled to get out of the car, he had flowers in his hand. His hospice nurse, Patricia, had asked him whether he wanted to bring flowers to his wife, since he was going home for dinner. He was able to say yes, and so she took him to purchase some. She preserved his dignity even in the midst of great physical weakness.

Dignity also matters greatly in workplace situations. Senior diplomats tell me that if you challenge someone publicly, you challenge their dignity. The resulting embarrassment often results in intense anger and defensiveness that makes agreement challenging. Diplomats who are skilled in negotiation know that if they need to have a difficult conversation, they have it one-on-one. One diplomat described a major multinational negotiation that broke down in the middle of the night due to a leader feeling his dignity had been insulted: "He left the building in anger. I followed him to see what was happening and, away from the negotiation room, I told him I honored his need and wanted to help. Eventually he returned. Supporting his dignity saved a major policy initiative that would have affected the entire globe."

Recognition is another big need in this category. I have seen the need for recognition come up in almost *every single one* of the many hundreds of cases I have mediated over the course of my career. Many of the relationship cases I assist are, at their core, about each person's need to be recognized for what they bring to the relationship. Likewise, in business situations, when people feel that they or their views are not recognized, negotiations and organizations break down. If one of the decision-makers sufficiently acknowledges each viewpoint, she may well get people on board even if all their views do not make it into the initiative under consideration.

Finally, most people in negotiation care deeply about their reputation. Over the course of many negotiations, I've seen reputation come up over and over again as a critical need, one that often stays below the surface unless you recognize it. Many people who consult with me on negotiating their salary tell me that the money, in addition to providing the necessities of life, also helps to build their reputation. If the negotiation you're approaching is the first of many similar ones you will need to tackle—for example, you're starting to negotiate with clients over your new product or service—you may find yourself concerned about your reputation as a company leader, or your product's reputation in the marketplace.

A talent agent recalled a story of trying to negotiate terms for one of the first actors he ever represented. The agent was new, and realized he was showing inflexibility and exasperating the production company. But he pressed on. Why? He was just starting out and didn't want to be known as a soft negotiator. If reputation seems like it might be a need for you in your negotiation (and it often is), take a moment to consider it now.

Self-direction needs, including freedom or autonomy. People have a deep need to know that they are in charge of making their own decisions to the extent possible under law, or the rules of an organization (this includes families!). Even if someone you're negotiating with, like a child, does not ultimately have decision-making power, consulting them and hearing them, or offering a menu of possible choices, can help satisfy these self-direction needs.

Together, these psychological and emotional needs dominate many of the legal, business, family, neighborhood, and diplomatic negotiations we encounter every day.

Other Needs

Rounding out our categories of needs are the following:

- **TRANSCENDENCE.** Values that transcend beyond the personal self (i.e., religious faith, mystical experiences and certain experiences with nature, service to others, aesthetic experiences, sexual experiences, the pursuit of science, etc.).
- **COGNITIVE.** Knowledge and understanding, curiosity, exploration, need for meaning, and predictability.
- **AESTHETIC.** Appreciation and search for beauty, balance, form, etc.
- **SELF-ACTUALIZATION.** Realizing personal potential and self-fulfillment, seeking personal growth and transformative experiences.

Recognizing my self-actualization needs led to the book you are reading today. Eighteen years ago, when I was a student at Columbia Law School, I sat down in a dingy New York City court conference room and experienced one of those transformative moments you normally see in movies. I had enrolled in a course called the Mediation Clinic, on the advice of a law school friend who said little more than "It involves talking a lot—you'll be great at it." My professors gave me a short mediation training course and then sent me down to court to mediate my first case.

That day, when the two parties sat down in front of me, and I started to help them resolve their dispute, I experienced a moment in which I realized, with perfect clarity, what I was put on this earth to achieve. I knew that when I was helping people negotiate better, I was realizing my highest potential. I felt more fulfilled than I'd ever felt before. The following semester, I went on to serve as a teaching assistant in the clinic and to help other students learn to mediate better. I absolutely loved it.

After graduating from Columbia Law School, I went to work as a lawyer at one of the nation's top law firms. I loved my work and my colleagues. I was well compensated. My parents were happy that I had found a stable job. But I yearned for more from my life. I thought back to that day in court and realized that I needed the fulfillment I had felt helping parties resolve their conflicts and students reach their own potential. I knew that returning to Columbia to teach mediation would allow me to grow. As I sit down to write this today, I know that recognizing my self-actualization needs led me to the best decision of my life—to leave a prestigious law firm job to teach and mediate. I wake up every day fulfilled by the work I'm doing.

We Prioritize Needs Differently

Note that while people generally prioritize their basic physical and safety needs above all else, this is by no means universal. Human beings value things differently; if you negotiate enough, you'll find, for example, some people who prioritize spiritual needs over economic security. I once mediated a legal case involving a religious organization. It was a breach of contract claim brought by the family of a deceased person against the religious organization to which he had belonged. The family alleged that the deceased, a loved one and a devoted member of this faith, had told them while he was alive that the organization had promised to bury him if he did not have enough money to cover his funeral expenses. When he died, the family contacted the organization to confirm that he was a congregant—but no one responded. Tearfully, the family told us that his body had sat in the morgue for a month until they could pull together the money to bury him.

There was no written contract in this case. But the organization's lawyer, herself a congregant of the same faith, told me from the beginning of the mediation that if what the family was alleging turned out to be true, the organization had a moral imperative to pay out a settlement no matter what the law said. The organization's spiritual needs trumped their economic or legal ones.

Going Further: Tangibles and Intangibles

Now that you've read these categories, which of these resonates with you? Do any additional needs come to mind? If so, go ahead and write those down, too.

Once you've completed your list, we'll take a closer look at what you've written down to help you achieve a deeper understanding of your needs. We'll formulate actionable steps you can take to ensure those needs are met. The first step is to take a look at your needs and categorize them by dividing them into two buckets: tangibles and intangibles.

Tangibles

Let's start with tangibles. Tangibles are things you can touch or feel or see or count: everything from clients, dollars, titles, or paintings to stores, scores, jobs, and units on a shelf. So if you ask yourself, "What do I need?" and start out by answering with tangible items, like "more money," "a promotion to vice president," or "new clients," that's a great place to start. Make sure you have covered all the tangibles you can identify.

But that's not where our work ends today, because we want to go beyond the tangible when considering your needs. Look at the tangibles on your list and ask yourself these follow-up questions:

"What makes this important?"
"What does this represent for me?"

These questions help you get at why you need the tangibles you've listed. Once we know the *why*, we can move on in subsequent chapters to tackle the *how*. For example, you might start with something concrete like, "I need five new clients this quarter." When you ask yourself what makes this important, you might find yourself realizing "I need more clients because that means greater financial security," or "I need a sense of challenge and advancement in my life." That's great. Once you've drilled down past the concrete, you uncover your deepest needs and values. We will use those to design your solution.

Tangibles often represent something else—something larger, of which the tangibles are just a part. We need to get underneath the tangibles to figure out the larger needs that lie underneath. For example, when I asked Walden, the CEO of a wellness consumer product start-up, about his needs for his company, one of the first things that came up was "achieve penetration into major chain stores and then achieve velocity (rate of customer consumption) in certain Midwest cities by 1Q2021." When I followed up and asked him why this was important, he replied, "Everyone knows our product can succeed on the coasts. Many new wellness products do great in New York and LA. That's a given. What distinguishes the products that succeed is high uptake in the rest of the country. If we achieve high velocity rates in cities like Des Moines, for example, our investors and the market will know we are here to stay, and we'll set ourselves up for the next round of financing." I summarized this back for him and asked him, "So what does the Midwest penetration number really mean for your needs?" He said, "Well, I hadn't thought about this, but really, the Midwest number means investment—keeping the investors we have happy and attracting new ones." We added "Investor Attraction/Satisfaction" to our list of needs, and put the "Midwest numbers" underneath it.

Like Walden, once you make those deeper needs explicit, you may end up expanding or refining the tangibles that go with it. After you identify why those are important to you, I want you to ask yourself, "How else might I fulfill my need for investor satisfaction?" In this way, you'll both clarify the root need and generate a complete list of options to meet it.

Intangibles

Some of the needs on your list may be intangibles, which are ephemeral but important ideals that give our lives meaning—like many of the needs we discussed earlier in this chapter. When you listed your tangible needs above and then connected them to something deeper, those deeper needs are your intangibles. Some common intangibles include respect, reputation, acknowledgment, communication, success, progress, love, security, privacy, and freedom.

Sometimes intangibles can feel fuzzy or soft because you can't see or count them. But intangibles are important because they usually transcend any one particular issue and give meaning and purpose to our lives as a whole. Recognizing these intangible needs can help you chart a course for your entire professional or personal life. Remember that in this book we are steering your relationships and your future for the long haul, not just this one negotiation. You're uncovering your personal needs in a way that will create value far beyond one handshake, contract, or hug.

So if you don't yet have any intangibles on your list, take a moment and think about the needs you have listed. Do any of them connect to one of the intangibles you've seen in this chapter? Do any other intangibles occur to you as you're reading this?

And if you already have intangibles, great. Now we want to do the second phase of our work: concretize them. We want to make those intangible needs actionable so that you can start the work of moving toward realizing them. So for each of these intangibles, you are going to ask yourself an important follow-up question:

What would that look like?

For example, when mediating business conflicts, I often hear people say, "I need a fair resolution to this issue." They repeatedly bring up fairness. When I ask, "What would fairness look like for you here?" that's where we start making progress toward a solution. Fairness can look vastly different for different people. When I have asked people this question, here is just a sampling of what I've heard in response:

$200,000

$2,000

a promotion

help setting up a child's speech therapy appointments

mentorship from a C-suite executive

an hour of television on weekend days

a discount on future dry cleaning

voting rights

time off

time away without the kids

removal of six feral cats from a residential property (yes, really)

a better office location

an apology

Getting the picture? Fairness may mean different things to *you* in different contexts, or at different times. You'll never know until you ask. So for each of your intangibles, make sure you have asked yourself, "What would that look like?" Once you have your initial answers, make sure your list is complete by asking yourself, "How else might I achieve fairness (or whatever it is that I need) in this situation?" Keep going until you have what feels like a complete list.

As another example: Brett has been thinking about going back to work after ten years at home with her three boys, who are now nine, seven, and five years old. Formerly a management consultant and project manager, she has grown interested in nutrition consulting and has taken a few courses while at home raising her kids. She knows she wants to start her own business, and she's generated a devoted social media following. But for some time, Brett has found herself torn about which direction to take, and now finds herself feeling stalled. She has decided to write down her needs in the hope that this will give her clarity about her work ambitions.

On her list she included "a sense of progress." When I asked Brett what "a sense of progress" would look like, she answered, "Hmm, I think producing something tangible that people can consume. Maybe creating a PDF with tips that I could hand out. And seeing in-person clients. I don't just want a social media platform. Having people actually work with me, in person or over Skype, would feel like progress." Thanks to my question, we were able to identify more about her needs (as well as steps she could take to fulfill them): producing something tangible that people can see or hold in their hands, and finding clients to work with her.

What About Money?

Economic needs are real. Money counts as one of the basic, tangible human needs because it allows us to buy the necessities of life. But money also represents other things. In that way, it can also be an intangible; it is a proxy for respect, acknowledgment, progress, contribution, achievement, and even freedom.

Over the years I've spoken to many people from different industries who have told me about financial negotiations they simply couldn't close even when the terms they offered were objectively reasonable, or even great. Why does this happen? Because often the number isn't tied to damages or economic realities as much as it symbolizes something else for that person. The need for recognition. A desire for fairness. Heartbreak over a failed relationship.

So if money comes up as a tangible, explore what that money means to you. What value does it represent? And how else, in addition to money, might you achieve that value? If money comes up as an intangible, like "economic freedom," ask yourself, "What would economic freedom look like?" This will help you place the money in its proper context and give you information on exactly what you need in order to achieve that value. Is it a flourishing retirement fund? One year's salary in savings?

Knowing what you actually need will help you design your future in a way that goes far beyond the outcome of one individual negotiation.

Troubleshooting Common Problems

Here are some additional tips to help you through a few possible issues when answering "What do I need?":

What If I'm Stuck?

What if you've read this far and you're still drawing a blank? If you're having trouble identifying any needs, I have two tricks that often help. Here is the first:

TIP ONE: THINK ABOUT WHAT YOU ARE CURRENTLY FINDING INTOLERABLE ABOUT YOUR SITUATION OR WHAT'S UPSETTING YOU MOST, THEN FLIP IT AROUND AND WRITE DOWN ITS OPPOSITE. That's your need. For example, if one of your main issues is feeling undervalued in your relationship, what you're seeking might be appreciation, respect, or recognition. If you are sitting down with this book because of a job that doesn't allow you a moment of rest or peace . . . well, now you can see what you need.

TIP TWO: SEPARATE YOURSELF FROM WHAT OTHER PEOPLE THINK OR BELIEVE YOU SHOULD NEED. It's easy to get caught up in what *other people* have told us we need or what we think we *should* need based on what others have. If you're stuck because you're thinking about someone else and what they think you need, go ahead and address that. Make a list of everything that person thinks you should need—then literally put it aside. Having it written out in front of you will help you separate what you need versus what you've been told you should need.

How Do I Think about My Needs If I'm Negotiating on Behalf of Someone, or an Organization?

"What do I need?" can be used for companies or institutions, as well as people. Once we've done our initial brainstorming on needs, I like to get deeper by helping you break out your needs according to the different roles or identities you bring to the table—or what I call "hats."

How do we make sure we have accounted for all our different "hats" or roles? Think about your (1) responsibilities; (2) identities; and (3) roles, formal or informal. For example, Keisha, a teacher and the mother of a girl with autism, is negotiating with a school district over her daughter Imani's IEP (an educational plan for children with disabilities). When she sits at the table, she's thinking about her needs as (1) a parent to Imani, who can't articulate her own needs; (2) a leader of the local special education parent-teacher organization, who works on behalf of all children in the town; and (3) an educator who values the role and expertise of teachers. Recognizing all these needs helped Keisha decide both what she wanted to advocate for (a personal aide for Imani and daily therapies) and how she needed to frame her arguments to resonate for the teachers in the room.

Likewise, if you are acting on behalf of an organization, you will have institutional needs as well as personal needs, as Lilia did in the story that began this chapter.

In summary, when we parse out all the identities that people bring to the table when they negotiate, it serves several purposes: first, it allows us to expand our list of needs so we can achieve the fullest possible picture of what we need from a negotiation. Second, it helps us identify the different roles we occupy as we negotiate, some that may not have even occurred to us. Last, it may help us pinpoint interests that appear to conflict—and I find that internally conflicting needs are a main cause of conflict and stagnation.

What If Some of My Needs Appear to Conflict?

As you uncover your needs, you may find that some of them appear to conflict. For example, if you are considering changing jobs from a large, established company to a start-up, you might simultaneously need the professional growth that comes from bringing a new product to market and the need to maintain financial stability for your family. This is a great discovery! It might give you a clue as to why you've been unable to take steps toward the job decision. Write both needs down. Once we know that you have possibly conflicting needs—and many of us do—then we can figure out whether they actually conflict, or whether there's a mutually satisfying path forward. Hint: there usually is.

If you have opened this book because you feel a sense of personal or professional stagnation, look through your list of needs and ask yourself whether any of them appear to clash. If so, this can give rise to a sense of internal conflict that can result in (1) a stalled out feeling, and (2) conflicting feelings or behaviors. One way to tackle this is to look at the needs you think conflict and concretize them to see if that's really the case.

Breaking out our needs into our roles, identities, or "hats" can also illuminate conflicts. Think back to Brett, who is considering going back to work after some time at home with her boys but has found herself torn about which direction to take. She feels as though she's at odds with herself. When we talked about her "hats" and her needs, she broke it down as follows:

PARENT	SPOUSE	FOR MYSELF
Connection with my boys	Financial balance with my husband	Connection with others
Help son with reading	Making house run smoothly	Financial contribution
Invest in their development	Peace in home	Sense of progress
Be there when they are little	Connection with husband	Adventure

After we laid it out this way, Brett took a look at her needs and said, "I'm concerned that my need for connection with my boys may conflict with my desire for travel and adventure." We then took a look at each of these interests to see what they might look like in practice.

When Brett asked herself what "connection with my boys" looked like, she discovered that for her it was:

- Having dedicated time that is devoted to each of them
- Saturday-morning snuggles before sports and activities
- Family dinner twice a week with no screens

When we addressed her desire for "travel and adventure," she defined this as:

- A trip once a year that is "just for her," without family
- Hosting a workshop in another city that she runs for other women who also value travel and community
- Taking a French class
- Doing something that takes her out of her comfort zone

When we look at these two lists, do these two interests actually conflict? Or are there ways for Brett to achieve both? When Brett and I looked at this list, we immediately saw that there were many ways in which she could satisfy both of these very important interests, at least most of the time. For example, she could take a weekly class and also find time to have a screen-free family dinner twice a week. She could cuddle with her boys, have date nights with her spouse, and also plan a personal trip or retreat that would fulfill her. Sometimes we might find ourselves with a hard conflict between interests—for example, a need for a new, updated kitchen might collide with a need to build up one's savings and emergency fund—but very often if we drill down and examine what our needs actually look like in practice, we find there's a way to achieve both of them.

(And get ready, you're going to do this exercise of harmonizing needs all over again once you ask someone else about theirs, in the Window section.)

A Final Note on Needs: Like Humans, They Evolve

As Anaïs Nin tells us, "Life is a process of becoming." Needs, like the people who own them, are never static: they are always shifting and changing. As we change, our identities and roles change, too. So our needs as sons, women, managers, doctors, and coaches will all evolve as we do.

My needs as a faculty member are different now than they were when I started at Columbia twelve years ago. Walden's needs as his company's CEO will be different at the beginning, when he's refining his product and seeking seed money, than when his company is doing its third round of financing and expanding nationwide. Brett's needs as a parent, as a spouse, and as a person will change as she evolves and her children grow and develop.

So if you have an ongoing issue that requires multiple negotiations, your needs may evolve during that time, too. If you're meeting with the other person more than once, meet with yourself, then, too.

Wrap-Up ... and One Final Question

Here is one more quick exercise for you. I want you to take a moment now to admit to what you haven't yet acknowledged.

What does that mean? Sometimes the greatest needs we have are the ones we hide even from ourselves. We self-censor without even knowing it. So I want you to finish this chapter by pausing and asking yourself this question: *What is the worst, least flattering thing (or things) I could possibly need in this situation?*

When I asked Brett this question, after having heard her more "socially acceptable" needs to take care of her family and nourish her relationship with her husband, she paused, took a breath, and then unearthed some of her "secret" needs. Eventually, she admitted that she needs a feeling of achievement beyond the home. "I know I shouldn't be focused on this so much . . . I'm a mom, right? My kids are the most important, of course. But I really miss feeling that I'm *achieving* something in the larger world."

This exercise in listing our "worst" possible needs is important for everyone. We often censor what we need. We think it's not nice or appropriate to need a sense of achievement, attractiveness . . . or money. What is so wrong about these needs? Why does this feel hard to admit? When we ignore these needs, we end up denying a piece of who we are, limiting what we achieve in negotiation—and stifling who we could become.

Now that you've answered this question, tried on all your "hats," listed your tangibles and intangibles, and followed up to go deep and get concrete, we're going to wrap up by summarizing your needs. Review everything you've written and jot down a one-paragraph summary. Take note of any words or themes that keep coming up for you. You'll use this summary as you move forward.

THREE

WHAT DO I FEEL?

Cara was a busy senior executive at a major international consumer products company, who was known for her dry sense of humor and no-nonsense personality. There for eighteen years, since she graduated college, she had advanced steadily up the ranks by selling household cleaners and personal care products to major drugstore chains and other stores.

The job was fast-paced and stressful at times. But during Cara's entire tenure at the company, even her closest colleagues and friends had never seen her get upset or shed a tear. She was often heard to say, "I don't get upset. I don't have time to get upset." In her yearly reviews, the main constructive criticism she received was to "slow down." As she grew in seniority at work, she married and saved rigorously, living on much less than her salary and taking very little financial risk in order to buy her dream home, with plenty of savings to spare. When it came time for her to purchase a home, she showed me the impressive Excel spreadsheet she had built of all her desired features and that analyzed which homes met which criteria. "I make a spreadsheet for everything," she said. She chose the home with the most check marks on the sheet.

Eventually Cara went on to have two boys. After they were born, she grew passionate about healthy living, and pursued a nutrition certification. As she turned her attention to feeding her family healthy meals, she also started thinking more about what kinds of household products she wanted to use with them, and started investigating more natural options. She compared the products she used at home to the products she was selling at work and saw a disconnect. She started to think it might be time to make a move.

For the last year, Cara had been looking at start-up companies in the natural cleaning products space, waiting for the right opportunity to present itself. Lots of companies were interested in hiring her. She consulted with me as a negotiation coach throughout her search—assessing market power, deal terms, and leadership team profiles for each potential company in an expansive Excel spreadsheet—only to reject each offer and move on. Finally, one offer came along that had some advantages over the others. The company was in the right market and stage of development, with the right title, but the financial package would represent a pay cut from her salary at the stable giant in her field. She went back and forth for several weeks, negotiating terms and debating whether to move. Finally, she reached a decision point: she had gotten as much as she could from the job negotiations, both in terms of money and information about the company's future prospects, and now she needed to make a decision. But she felt paralyzed. "I've analyzed everything I possibly can," she told me. "But for some reason I can't bring myself to decide one way or the other." The start-up told her she had one more week to let them know whether she was taking the job.

It was at this point that Cara mentioned in passing, during one of our consulting calls, that she hadn't been able to get out of bed that morning. In fact, she'd needed to put her gym membership on hold; she'd been dealing with debilitating muscle pain for months, to the point of rendering her bedridden on several occasions. Her doctors had run every test they could think of, and all came up negative. And today, the pain prevented her from even making breakfast.

This was my opening. I took a breath and asked, "What are you feeling about this decision?" My no-nonsense client, who had run every comparative metric possible without once mentioning what I jokingly call "the F-word," finally opened up and allowed herself to contemplate the feelings she was experiencing over this decision. She had known that moving to a start-up would involve a pay cut, and she had prepared for years in order to manage the hit to their finances. But she hadn't anticipated how much anxiety she would feel about leaving the sure bet that had seen her through the last eighteen years, in exchange for a financial risk that could affect her family in the short term—though with hopes for a longer-term payout. She also couldn't ignore the intense feeling of guilt that, at her current job, she wasn't selling products she would use with her own kids. She told me that recently the company had developed a product she really didn't believe in, and nonetheless, she had to get on the phone with potential buyers and sell it. She would hang up nauseated after every call.

Writing these feelings down in her spreadsheet was clarifying for her. She examined her monetary anxiety against the numbers: she was able to remind herself that she was amply prepared for the short-term salary reduction and that through her research about the start-up, she had amassed solid evidence that she would end up making more money once it was acquired. She realized that this financial anxiety was natural but would likely be temporary. The anticipation of the hit might even be worse than the reality of it.

Then she came to her guilt about the products she was currently selling. She knew that this guilt, unlike the financial anxiety, was likely to persist until she worked for a company that was more in line with her values. She realized that, in fact, this guilt had been growing within her for years. She couldn't continue to sell products to families that she didn't feel good about using with her own kids.

This executive, who prepared meticulously for this job negotiation and analyzed all the pieces of hard data available to her, hadn't even realized she first needed to negotiate with herself over the feelings she was experiencing about the decision. Armed with this additional information about her feelings, she made the call: she took the job. The pain cleared up almost immediately. One year later, she was beating even the optimistic sales benchmarks her new company had set for her. She told me that she attributed this success in large part to her happiness at work. Her belief in the products led her to sell with a level of enthusiasm and energy she hadn't experienced in years.

"Feelings Are Facts"

When I first studied negotiation, my mentor, Carol Liebman, taught me that feelings are facts. She did not mean to say that feelings are as objective a reality as time, weight or temperature, but rather that they are real, they exist, and they must be dealt with in any negotiation. Feelings shape our perception of reality and our decision-making at every turn.

We can't prevent ourselves from experiencing feelings in negotiation. I once read an article that astutely compared human emotion to a volcano. Volcanoes are generative: they create islands that eventually bear plant and animal life. But they can also be destructive. Lava flow can destroy property and life itself. As with volcanoes, you can't stop human emotions from erupting. But with preparation, you can direct the lava flow into the sea instead of the village, thereby maximizing the benefit and minimizing any damage.

We often try to bury our feelings or deny that they exist, but I have always found (and research supports) that this practice tends to be more destructive than helpful, and that it can be more productive to face them. When we hold a Mirror to our feelings, two things happen: first, we clear away the fog or confusion that surrounds a conflict or important decision, leaving us feeling more organized and empowered; and second, we find information that helps us solve our issue.

In this chapter, I will help you identify any feelings you are experiencing about your negotiation. Along the way, we'll talk about why feelings are central to negotiation, and how identifying them can help you negotiate more effectively. I will help you listen to your internal voice non-judgmentally so that you can write down your actual feelings, not the ones your mother thinks you should be feeling. Together, we'll follow up on your initial thoughts to make sure you've considered everything you might be feeling. And I will give you strategies for how to handle your feelings once you enter the Window phase and are talking face-to-face with someone else.

First, as always, the preparation starts at home, with you.

Your Turn in the Mirror

Now it's your turn to look in the Mirror. Remember, you've already identified what's brought you here, as well as your needs. You have a sense of the problem you want to solve and what you need from the situation. Now you're going to get into your feelings. As you did in the other chapters, I want you to get into a physical space where you can think freely. For the next five minutes, think about and write down your answer to the question *What do I feel?*

Dealing with the "F-Word" in Negotiation

In this chapter, we will talk about feelings, or what I sometimes call "the other F-word," in negotiation. Sometimes people are caught off-guard to talk about feelings while they're on the job, or even in their personal negotiation.

This hesitation makes sense. For years, the conventional wisdom about feelings in negotiation was that feelings—whether positive or negative—are unproductive. We should just try not to have them, or if we do, we should stuff them down and negotiate on the facts.

But grappling with your feelings is the key to success in any negotiation. What makes feelings so essential? Two important factors:

1. **FEELINGS ARE ALWAYS PRESENT IN NEGOTIATION**
   Remember that any conversation in which you're steering a relationship is a negotiation. You are constantly negotiating as you

manage your relationships with colleagues, clients, managers, your spouse or partner, children, and the person who rear-ended your car on the road last week. A relationship is a moment (or longer) of connection between you and another human being or group. As a human being, you can also have a relationship with yourself.

Any relationship or connection that involves humans, no matter how businesslike or brief, involves feelings. We're used to thinking about feelings insofar as they affect our so-called personal lives, like in the context of our family relationships, but we often fail to appreciate that feelings are present in *all* negotiations. (If at some point we're all replaced by computers, this may be a different story.) It doesn't matter what kind of issue you're facing, whether you are at the table negotiating on behalf of someone else or an institution, or whether you're normally what one might call an "emotional person." If your negotiation involves people (i.e. you), it's personal, and feelings will be part of it.

If feelings are always there, doesn't it make sense to acknowledge and work with them?

2. **FEELINGS DIRECTLY IMPACT OUR DECISION-MAKING AND OTHER ABILITIES IN NEGOTIATION**

Feelings are important in negotiation because our feelings help us make decisions, big and small. Neuroscientist Antonio Damasio studied a number of patients whose right side of the brain (which controls emotions) was impaired, but who otherwise were cognitively intact, and found that they were unable to make decisions. They could talk through what they logically thought they should do, but couldn't even decide what to eat for dinner. Without the ability to make decisions, we would be lost in negotiation.

Emotions also affect innovation and creativity: psychology research has found that positive emotions, like compassion or gratitude, can enhance our ability to judge circumstances accurately, come up with creative solutions, and innovate—all of which are important for negotiation. Negative emotions, especially fear and anxiety (we'll talk about each of these later in this chapter), can inhibit these abilities. Acknowledging our feelings and treating them like any other kind of data to consider in negotiation can help us make the most of this connection between emotion and action.

The Importance of Feelings in Professional Negotiations

People sometimes express doubt that so-called professional negotiations—negotiations you do at work or maybe on behalf of an organization, like a company or a government—can involve feelings. But if you want to be a dealmaker in business, diplomacy, or any other field, you will need to understand and deal with feelings. Andra Shapiro, an executive vice president and general counsel for Cable Entertainment at NBCUniversal, negotiates deals in order to bring the very best programming to people all around the world. One of her most common negotiations involves making deals with people like writers and producers who create original content on any number of networks and platforms, to purchase or license their work.

Andra says that you'd think their negotiations only deal with money, and it's true that economics are present in virtually every deal, but you'd be surprised at how often emotions are at the center of the negotiations, especially with content creators. "When we negotiate with someone over the things they've created, it's as though they are handing over their *baby* to you," she observes. "It's extremely emotional and you have to respect that, understand that, or you will not do successful deals in this space."

Likewise, when business deals go bad, a surprising percentage of those disputes arise because of unexamined feelings. One lawyer with mediation training told me about an experience he had as a partner at a major firm. His client, a large U.S. player in the health-care industry, was acquired by an even larger foreign giant. The acquisition process went smoothly until the two CEOs went to the closing dinner. There, they had an enormous fight fueled by cultural differences, wine, and insecurity over their future roles within the combined organization—which resulted in the American CEO calling his lawyer late at night on a Friday to say, "I want you to draft an arbitration complaint immediately. We're going to sue the #@$% out of this $%@!"

The lawyer listened to what his client had to say. But he also knew that the arbitration complaint would likely be both unsuccessful and expensive. So, remembering his mediation training and sensing the emotional issue at stake, he spent the weekend alternately drafting the complaint and talking to his client, asking him, "Okay, so tell me more about the dinner . . ." (Note: You'll find that question in the Window section.) In the end, the lawyer helped his client get some emotional space and perspective on what happened at the closing dinner. The CEO ended up dropping his request for the arbitration complaint, instead refocusing his energy on making the combined company a success.

Looking in the Mirror: The Benefits of Considering Your Feelings

The best way to prepare for and deal with feelings in negotiation is to identify your own. Thinking about your feelings helps you in several ways.

First, it gives you important data you can use when you negotiate. Negotiation is not only driven by what we need or believe on a certain issue, but how strongly we feel about it. Knowing how you feel about an issue will help you understand how much you want to prioritize it in negotiation. Take a moment to look over your feelings and see what they tell you about how you should approach your Window conversation with the other person.

Second, recognizing your feelings may help you to craft better solutions. One magic follow-up question can help you turn feelings into future-focused ideas. If you are feeling a negative emotion, I want you to ask yourself, "What would help eliminate or reduce my [*insert feeling*] in this situation?" For example, if you are a doctor going through this chapter and you discover that your overwhelming emotion is frustration about the way you are required to provide care to a certain patient population in your hospital, I want you to ask yourself, "What would help eliminate or reduce my frustration in this situation?" In this way, you can use your feelings to generate concrete ideas for how to move forward.

Last, acknowledging and expressing your feelings privately will help reduce the chance that you feel or express them in an uncontrollable way during the part of the negotiation where you sit down with another person. Research shows that if we stuff down our emotions, they may boomerang back at a moment or in a way that impedes our ability to make decisions, or clouds how we approach the decision. Again, you can't keep that feelings volcano from erupting, but acknowledging your feelings and preparing yourself to handle them in a negotiation will help you harness their power and achieve great results.

Considering Your Feelings Brings Relief, and Results

Stephen is a senior partner at a large U.S. law firm. As he has grown more established in his practice and closer to retirement, his firm has asked him to take on increased responsibility with recruiting new talent and mentoring them into partner positions. Eight years ago, he brought in a young real estate lawyer, Craig, who showed the promise of being a brilliant contributor to the firm. Stephen mentored Craig in a junior partner position, celebrating Craig's strengths and also counseling him on areas to improve. What Stephen noticed, however, was that Craig, who was brilliant at generating new clients, sometimes moved too quickly and disregarded firm paperwork and protocol. One day, Stephen received a difficult call; his firm's managing partner called him to say that Craig had brought in a new client with a real estate issue that required filing a lawsuit in court. Firm policy dictated that every complaint filed in court needed to include the name of, and be reviewed by, someone who was (1) a senior equity partner and (2) from the litigation department. Craig was not a litigator, nor was he a senior equity partner. He knew about this policy and yet he filed the complaint himself anyway.

Stephen reviewed the complaint. Craig's work was very good. But had he consulted Stephen, or someone else in the litigation department, his work could have been slightly more comprehensive. And management was angry at what they saw as deliberate disregard of firm policy. Stephen pulled out the Mirror questions to start working through them. He knew what he needed: to ensure Craig followed firm policy from now on, while also keeping Craig at the firm and motivated to continue generating clients. Stephen also needed to preserve their good working relationship. Finally, as a litigator, Stephen felt a responsibility to make sure this client achieved a good result in court.

When he got to "What do I feel?" things got interesting for Stephen. He listed a few emotions that felt relatively obvious:

- Anxiety about the conversation
- Fear of making things worse between Craig and management
- Annoyance at Craig for not following the policy
- Relief at the prospect of getting this sorted out

But then, as he thought about it, he wrote down a couple more:

- Empathy for Craig
- Ambivalence about the policy

This surprised Stephen. Writing down his feelings made him realize two things. First, he realized that he could understand what happened here for Craig. Stephen, like Craig, was excellent at building relationships with new clients and solving their problems—fast. He could see himself in Craig, and deep down, he felt Craig's intentions were to help, rather than to hurt the firm. He wrote all this down so he could include it when he spoke to Craig.

Second, Stephen discovered that he wasn't sure the firm's bright-line policy made sense. He realized that to fully solve the problem, he might need to pursue parallel tracks: one with Craig and one with management, to see whether they might build any flexibility into the policy, or be willing to brainstorm other ideas to help their junior partners.

Sometimes we fear that if we look in the Mirror to see our feelings, it might somehow make our situation worse. But far from hurting his negotiation, taking a few minutes to consider his feelings helped Stephen to connect with Craig, flesh out the actual problem(s) to be solved more fully, and craft some steps forward. If you work through this question the way Stephen did, you'll likely find the same is true for you.

Find the Fun

One final note about looking in the Mirror for feelings. Often, when prompted to consider their feelings in negotiation, people approach it with a bit of dread. It's as though I'm asking, "What unpleasant things do you feel?" And they answer accordingly by writing down all the negative things that come to mind. So I want to follow up with a specific prompt: Have you written down positive feelings that come to mind? If not, do that now.

I want to encourage you to get in touch with your positive feelings for every negotiation you encounter. Too often we allow our negative emotions to predominate over our negotiations, but underneath those feelings we also have some really positive feelings about the negotiations we encounter. Yes, you're nervous about pitching a client or approaching a conversation with your partner. But couldn't you also be excited to get this next phase of your career started? Might you be relieved at the prospect of getting off the mental hamster wheel of this conflict to clear the air with someone? I recently took a roomful of executives through this question. One participant, facing a major financial negotiation with an employee, wrote down "frustration that she is not realistic about the numbers," and then "excited to push my skills as a negotiator." "Finding the fun" (or joy, pride, excitement, or triumph) can help us consider the full picture of how we feel about our negotiation, and summon the energy to tackle it.

Following Up: Navigating Issues with Feelings

We've established why it makes sense to consider feelings as part of any negotiation, and we've worked through the question itself. Next, we'll troubleshoot any issues you might experience when thinking about your feelings. Let's take a look at a few common speed bumps, and I'll give you ways to overcome them.

1. **"I CAN'T FEEL THINGS WHILE I'M WEARING A SUIT."**

    Are you asking yourself about your feelings in a place where you can be honest about the answers? The first time I ever previewed these questions at the United Nations, I was surprised by how many diplomats, male and female, teared up *immediately* upon my asking this question, and then had trouble allowing themselves to write anything down. One of them said, "I'm not used to asking myself about feelings while wearing a suit. What I feel at work is only what I want to allow myself to feel. The things I'm thinking about aren't 'suit feelings.'"

    I've come to understand that a lot of us really need to talk about our emotions, but don't allow ourselves the opportunity. Instead, we try to shut off our feelings, especially in the workplace. It doesn't matter whether you wear a suit, uniform, or the same pair of shorts every day to work. If you're thinking about this question at work and are having trouble, try getting yourself to a place where you can explore your non-suit feelings.

2. **"I DON'T KNOW. I'M STUCK."**

    What if you're stuck and can't figure out what you feel at all? Perhaps you've asked yourself this question and now you're drawing a blank.

    We have the ability to think about our emotions, but that doesn't mean we always have an easy time identifying or expressing them. We are so used to suppressing our emotions—or on the flip side, feeling overwhelmed by them—that sometimes it can be difficult to identify with specificity what we are feeling. I've included several strategies here for identifying your emotions when you feel stuck.

Common Human Emotions

If you're stuck figuring out how you feel, take a look at the list below of the most common emotions. While human beings experience a broad range of feelings—a greater number than we can capture in this chapter—we also commonly experience some of the same emotions, especially in negotiation or conflict. Dr. Brené Brown and other psychology experts have worked on devising groups of core emotions that we can examine and use in our own lives. Below you will find a list of emotions that commonly arise in negotiations, some of which were identified by these experts, and some of which I have identified through my own experience coaching thousands of people through negotiations:

Admiration	Empathy	Pride
Anger	Excitement	Rage
Anxiety	Fear	Regret
Appreciation	Frustration	Rejection
Belonging	Gratitude	Relief
Betrayal	Grief	Sadness
Blame	Guilt	Satisfaction
Calm	Happiness	Shame
Compassion	Horror	Stress
Confusion	Humiliation	Surprise
Contempt	Hurt	Sympathy
Curiosity	Jealousy	Triumph
Desire	Joy	Vulnerability
Disappointment	Judgment	Worry
Disgust	Loneliness	
Embarrassment	Love	

Once you've reviewed this list, feel free to make any additions or adjustments you need to the one you generated earlier.

For Feelings, Go Back to Your Needs

If you're having trouble coming up with feelings, try going back to your needs. Often your needs and your feelings are flip sides of the same coin. Turn back to chapter 2 and look again at the intangible or tangible needs you discovered. Very often, what people are feeling conflicted about is the opposite of those needs. If you need a better compensation package from your job, you might be feeling insecure, undervalued, or even upset that you're not getting what you feel you're worth. If you need more appreciation in your relationship, you might be feeling sad, angry, or just plain unappreciated. If you feel a desperate need for forward progress on your client list, you may be feeling stuck or left behind.

Identifying "the Worst Feeling": Combating Self-Censorship

Sometimes when I ask people what they are feeling, it turns out they are experiencing some feelings they are trying to hide, even from themselves. If you're having trouble coming up with how you feel, ask yourself, "What's the worst thing I could be feeling right now?" I love this follow-up question because a lot of the time we suppress our feelings to avoid shame or self-judgment. We don't want to be feeling them. We wish they were something else. So we detach from those feelings. Except, stuffing them down or denying them doesn't make them go away. Shining a light on our "worst" feelings (which I place in quotes because feelings are not bad or good, they just *are*), even if they seem unattractive, reduces their effect on us and helps lighten our emotional load. Once we hold up a Mirror to some of these feelings, we're in a much clearer place from which to move forward.

The Big Two Hidden Emotions

Speaking of our "worst" feelings, I want to share with you the two most common feelings people feel but don't express when they are in conflict. I've seen these two emotions so many times I've lost count. We try to suppress them, but to no avail—they *always* come back up, like the monster at the very end of the action movie, causing havoc for the hero and heroine. What are they?

Guilt. And fear.

Guilt and fear are what I call the Big Two—the two emotions we avoid most, and the two emotions that blow up negotiations and relationships more than any other. I'm always reminded of the John F. Kennedy quote: "Let us never negotiate out of fear. But let us never fear to negotiate." When people seem difficult in a negotiation or relationship discussion, chances are they are feeling one of these emotions.

Last year I traveled around the United States to provide training for many of the regional offices of the Department of Education's Office for Civil Rights. These offices handle lawsuits filed by parents against school districts over aspects of their child's education—pretty intense stuff in terms of emotions. When I asked the civil rights investigators in one office to identify what they thought were the most common emotions parents might feel toward school districts, they generated a short list: anger, distrust, rage. I then asked them, "What would you say if I told you I thought most parents sitting in front of you were also feeling fear or guilt?"

There was a collective "Ohhhhhh," as eyes widened around the room. One participant said:

This makes so much sense. I bet the parents are feeling tons of guilt. Yes, the school district may have messed up, but could I have done better for my child? Why couldn't I solve this problem before we got here? And fear . . . that may be the number one emotion. Parents are scared their child's future may be ripped away depending on how they handle this one case. It makes them shut down and unable to negotiate. Now that I'm sitting here, I think a lot of the rage I've been seeing against the school district is really the parents' fear or guilt about the situation. And if we addressed that, maybe some of the rage would evaporate.

Think about this story about other people's feelings when you endeavor to tackle your own, and consider whether you might be dealing with the Big Two. Confronting feelings can be hard, right? Well, as a teacher, I believe in walking with you as we grapple with these challenging issues . . . so I'll go first. I'm going to tell you a story about my feelings and how my failure to recognize them almost damaged a close family relationship.

I grew up with a lawyer father I greatly admired and whose approval I always chased. Boisterous and somewhat combative, one of his colleagues described him to me as "the most pugnacious trusts and estates attorney I've ever met." I vividly recall at five years old asking my dad what a lawyer did and him telling me, "People come to Dad asking for advice. I tell them what I think they should do, and they give me their pennies and dimes." I thought that sounded like the best job in the world. (No surprise that I ended up going to law school twenty years later.)

I always longed for a closer relationship with my dad, one where we could talk more frequently or deeply about things that mattered. But my dad was never one for deep, emotional chats; he used to invent work reasons to call me, and then awkwardly transition to more personal talk with an "Um, so what else is new?" Our love of the law was one of our bonding points. When I won a major award at law school graduation, his beaming expression as they announced my name was worth more to me than the award itself.

Three years ago, my father, only seventy years old, became sick. Suddenly he went from seeming mildly apathetic and detached to forgetting my name and sending me emails with strings of unconnected words. My brothers and I feared a stroke. I called the Columbia Neurology department and brought my dad in for a series of memory tests. He failed all of them. The doctor told us we were dealing with a degenerative disease for which there was no cure and no treatment. My brothers and I coordinated the appointments and testing and worked together to cope with this devastating news.

My uncle Bill, Dad's lifelong best friend, confidant, champion, and only brother, has always been a second father to me. Since I was a teenager, I have called my "Unc" and aunt more times than I can count, for support and smart advice in a tough situation. This time, my uncle was part of the group of us who were dealing with this diagnosis, and so I didn't want to unload on him and make things worse. He similarly tried to spare me his own pain—and so for a period of time I felt we talked less than usual while each of us dealt with the news. The problem was, I started telling myself that this temporary space meant he wasn't happy about how I was handling my dad's treatment. This increased my fear. Was I up to this? Could I handle things better? Finally, at a family reunion where we were all confronted with how frail my dad was looking, my uncle asked an innocuous, offhand question about whether my dad's medications might need to be changed to help some of his symptoms. I lost it. I talked to my uncle and aunt angrily, without asking any questions first. I told them that my brothers and I were handling things now. That we knew what we were doing and had consulted the best doctors. That my dad was going to die of this disease and there was nothing any medication could do to stop it. And I walked off.

For the rest of the evening I felt terrible. A confusing mess of emotions surged inside me. When I took a moment to ask myself what I was feeling, what I discovered first was fear. I had been trying to project confidence, setting up meetings and asking all the right questions, but deep inside I was terrified about managing my dad's health care. In many respects I felt like a child again. I was scared to make such important decisions when I no longer had my dad—or now, my uncle—to ask for advice. Second, guilt. I secretly felt guilty that I couldn't do more for my dad to stop his suffering. I also felt awful that I had spoken to my loved ones in that way. I knew that they were terrified and grieving, just like I was. This fear and guilt made me defensive; I desperately needed my uncle and aunt's approval, but I'd gone about asking for it in the worst way possible.

My aunt approached me later in the evening and asked to talk. I'll always be grateful to her for this. We sat down on the stairs and she said, "You know . . . your uncle and I have never done this before, sitting back and watching the younger generation make decisions. We are feeling a little lost. But we have good intentions."

I said, "Thanks. You know, I've never done this before either. I'm also feeling lost. I've been freaking out on the inside. My dad is no longer able to tell me he approves of what I'm doing, so I really need to hear that you trust and support me."

She reassured me, "We do trust you. You and your brothers have done an amazing job with your dad. We didn't mean to question you by asking about the medication. Can we just assume the best of each other going forward?"

I agreed. "Definitely. I completely overreacted because I'm trying so hard to control a situation I can't control. Let's start over."

By confronting my own feelings and sharing them honestly with my aunt, each of us was able to recognize and honor each other's deep fear. We transformed a challenging family conflict into an opportunity to grow closer together. Today, my uncle and aunt are one of my main sources of support in a devastating time. My dad's doctors recently commented that they have rarely seen such a cohesive family unit. We all feel great sadness as my dad's condition worsens, but we find great comfort and relief in one another.

The Final Step: Expressing Your Emotions in Negotiation

So you've begun processing how you feel in order to prepare for negotiating. The next logical question is often, "Do I show that emotion when I sit down with the other person?"

As a general principle, I believe in transparency during negotiation.

Clear communication helps you create more value. And expressing positive emotions like compassion, excitement, or pride have been shown to help build a connection with the other party and increase the chance that they want to help you achieve your goals, as well as their own. But what about more negative emotions? I'll talk about the two that people ask about most—anger and anxiety—below.

Anger

Anger is a legitimate emotion, in life and in negotiation. Many people, especially women and people from certain cultures, are given the message that they should not feel or express anger, even though recognizing and expressing anger can generate empowering effects for many people.

But what do you do with that anger in negotiation? If you feel angry during a negotiation, research shows you may experience more difficulty coming up with creative, win-win solutions. You may also have more difficulty accurately assessing the needs of the person across from you (which we'll discuss in chapter 6). Addressing your anger in advance will help you communicate clearly and with intention when you do sit down with someone else.

Ultimately, the decision whether to show your anger in any given negotiation belongs to you. Displaying anger in negotiation has been shown to lead to mixed results. If you have more power than your counterpart, they may be more likely to make concessions in the short term as a result of your anger. But research shows that they may also be less likely to want to do business with you in the long term. If you have less power than your counterpart, showing anger may lead to escalation of the conflict and negotiation impasse.

For situations where you are angry but may not want to show your anger when you talk with someone else, expressing a milder emotion like disappointment may give you the chance to communicate that you are unhappy about something, while minimizing the likelihood of a reaction and maximizing your chances of achieving what you need from the negotiation.

Anxiety

Another tricky emotion to express in negotiation is anxiety. Anxiety in negotiation can lead people to accept flawed advice, give up easily, and ignore their own needs. If you've listed anxiety in your list of feelings from earlier in this chapter, in most cases you'll want to address this yourself instead of stating it out loud when you sit down with the other person. (The exception would be if this is a negotiation with someone close to you in your life, perhaps a family member or partner, in which one of the goals is complete transparency and closeness.)

When you address anxiety, it's important to consider whether you have anxiety about the substance of your negotiation (for example, how your salary compares to others in your department and what that means for your future at the company) or anxiety about the negotiation itself (such as the process of going to management to ask for more money).

Either way, you will benefit from acknowledging that anxiety and reflecting on it in advance. If you're feeling anxious about the substance of the conflict and you work through these questions before the negotiation, you'll have much more information that will help you feel prepared to tackle the negotiation. And if you feel anxious about the process of negotiating, you'll benefit even more from acknowledging and dealing with that anxiety. Recognizing that emotion and answering the other Mirror questions in this book will go a long way toward allaying the anxiety you feel about the negotiation itself. Negotiation always involves things we can't control, but there is also a lot that we can—and by asking yourself the right questions, you'll have tackled the part that's within your influence.

One final way to handle anxiety is to look at the Window questions in advance, and imagine what the other person might say in response. Write those answers down, and map out a potential strategy for when you ask the questions and then work to move the negotiation forward.

Wrapping Up

You've looked in the Mirror, confronted your feelings, and survived. Before we finish, take a moment to read through what you wrote down for this chapter, and summarize any important points or themes.

Next, we'll move on to a question that will help you generate excellent ideas for a solution to your issue—and feel great while doing it.

FOUR

HOW HAVE I HANDLED THIS SUCCESSFULLY IN THE PAST?

Even for smart, successful people, few negotiations bring up more unease and worry than asking for more money at work.

Andrew graduated from college three years ago with an undergraduate business degree and went to work for a financial institution. He wanted help negotiating for his first promotion, and an increased compensation package to go with it. From the moment Andrew arrived at the company, he launched himself into contributing not only to the bottom line but to the positive work environment by recruiting college students, mentoring them, and serving on a committee dedicated to employee well-being.

Andrew told me that when he first joined the company as an entry-level employee, the compensation was done in lockstep, which meant that everyone at that level was paid the same. You could still negotiate for good work assignments and mentors, but the money was the money. He worked hard and his work spoke for itself.

But three years in, Andrew wanted to become a manager. He had become eligible for promotion last year, but didn't advocate for it and hadn't been promoted. A child of immigrants, Andrew had been raised to believe that he wasn't entitled to anything, that hard work and dedication would lead to the best results. Now, however, he started to see he would need more than that in order to be successful. As his yearly review approached, Andrew hoped to use that occasion to make a case for his promotion, as well as a raise. He had a general sense that managers made 15–25 percent more than he was making right now, but the promotion—and his compensation—would depend on his advocacy. This year, he wanted to craft a strategy to ask for more.

We defined Andrew's main goal: he wanted to negotiate for as close to a 25 percent increase as possible. But he wanted more than that. He wanted to show management that he had what it took to be a future leader within the company. He also wanted to feel confident negotiating for himself, and not just on behalf of his company or clients. His needs included recognition of all he was doing for the company, including his client work and his institutional work; a sense that he was advancing toward senior partnership and perhaps company management; and more experience negotiating successfully for himself.

We also contemplated Andrew's feelings: On the one hand, he was excited to start actively managing his own career. On the other, he had mixed feelings about accumulating wealth for wealth's sake. At this point, he was making enough money to support himself and also help his parents out, too. He was comfortable negotiating on behalf of his company, but he felt slightly guilty about asking for more for himself. He acknowledged that these conflicting feelings had prevented him from asking for a raise or promotion last year, when he first became eligible.

I asked him how he had handled negotiations like this successfully in the past. He looked back at me and said, "This is the first time. During college, I interned for great companies, but all those positions were unpaid. Now I'm here. I work in finance, I'm doing very well, and yet I've never negotiated for my own compensation before. So I don't have a prior success to draw from here."

I looked back over my notes. "Okay. Let's look at the different elements of your approach and break it down. What do you think it's going to take for you to be successful here?"

He thought for a minute. "Well, I need to build a case, meaning that I'm going to need to review all the different aspects of my performance and cast them in the best possible light. I should also frame my arguments in terms that also make it clear that the company will benefit from promoting me and compensating me at a level I deserve. In my experience, this kind of approach works best with management, in addition to being consistent with my values. I should also spend some time talking individually to key players at my company, who can advocate for me when they make promotion decisions. Get them on board and give them the talking points they'll need to help make my case. Last . . . I'm going to need to kind of psych myself up to do this; like, really believing that I'm worth this much so that I can convince them of the same."

I summarized: "To be successful here, it sounds like you'll need to (1) research and build a case, (2) frame this as a mutual win, (3) get some key people on board, and (4) psych yourself up to believe that the outcome you're advocating is actually the right one, and not just the one you want. Let's look back through the past and see if there's a time you had a negotiation success involving those elements. You said earlier that you have experience with the company that indicated framing things as a mutual win would be most successful. Might that give us a clue as to where to start?"

Andrew thought about it and mentioned that as soon as he arrived at the company, he'd had the idea to start a training program for its junior employees, something that at the time was unique among competitive firms. His efforts led to a speaker series focused on mentoring junior employees in leadership, negotiation, and other skills that would help them advance. The program was extremely successful but had taken some advocating with the management team. Andrew had to make the case that it would help attract and retain top talent, which in turn would produce better PR and better financial results in the long term, since they'd have happier employees and less turnover. He had to frame it as a win for both junior ranks (including himself) and senior management.

Andrew explained his hesitation with doing the same thing this time around: "The one difference in this scenario is that I didn't have to advocate for just myself, so psyching myself up wasn't as much of an issue . . . But now that I'm thinking about it, I needed to advocate for myself in order to get this job in the first place. This is a competitive job market and a sought-after company to work for. I wasn't asking for specific compensation, but I was asking for a position, as well as the specific group I wanted, which had very limited openings. I believed I was a great fit for the job, that I could contribute here, and it showed. Maybe this negotiation isn't so different."

As a result of considering his prior negotiation success, Andrew came out of this conversation with concrete ideas for how he could approach this negotiation for his compensation. Six months later, he was a manager in his division, with two direct reports and an 18 percent compensation increase. But Andrew also got more than that. In the process of his individual conversations with management around the promotion, he shared that he was interested in rising to a senior management position eventually. One year later, he was placed on a company management committee that had only two spots for junior managers, a prestigious placement that signaled upper management's confidence in his leadership. He was on track to achieve his goals.

"How Have I Handled This Successfully in the Past?"

In this chapter, I want you to mine your past for ways in which you have successfully handled challenges similar to the one you face now. I will help you put yourself back in that successful mind-set so that you can access your inner wisdom and generate ideas that will help you move forward in your future negotiations. Considering a prior success will also make you feel more confident when you negotiate. And if, like Andrew, you can't recall a previous success in a similar situation, I'll help you find another success to help you tackle your current negotiation. Together, I know we'll discover that your prior success has more similarities to your current situation than you might expect. You'll finish this chapter with a clearer picture of your situation, ready to launch yourself into the future.

Considering a Prior Success

When I prompt people to consider a prior success, I often get to watch them transform before my eyes. They go from feeling unsure, apprehensive, or lost, to confident, organized, and even excited to negotiate. Asking about a prior success not only prepares you for the last question in the Mirror section but also helps get you ready for when it's time to sit down with someone else.

"How have I handled this successfully in the past?" is transformative for a few reasons. First, it places this one negotiation into context. When we experience an issue—a tough negotiation, a "no" from a prospective client, a relationship conflict, a collapsed business deal, or something we've never done before—we often dwell on that experience to the point that we forget about the many successes we've experienced in the past. Second, as in the example above, this question focuses us more specifically on approaches, circumstances, and techniques that have worked favorably for us, from which we can gather good data about what might work for us this time. Last—and most important—I know, both from research and experience, that when people spend time thinking about a previous success, they are more likely to achieve better results in their next negotiation. It's a powerful positive anchor. Together, we will help you use it to your advantage and launch you into your future in the best way possible.

Let's take each of these reasons in turn.

Placing Your Negotiation into Context

Sometimes, as with the executive above, we experience negative emotions around a negotiation—perhaps a conversation that didn't go well, one that is proving to be tougher than expected, or one that we haven't tackled yet but is making us anxious. This is especially true if your negotiation involves a long-term relationship, whether at work, at home, or with yourself.

If you are facing a negotiation that involves a long-standing person or issue in your life, and in chapter 3 you uncovered any negative emotions around your negotiation, this question will be helpful to you. When people encounter a conflict with someone they have known for a while, they sometimes allow that conflict to take up so much brain space (and with good reason!) that they forget they have handled a similar negotiation— or many similar negotiations—successfully in the past.

Let's take the situation of a doctor, Jamila, who was struggling with her long-time patient Ben. Ben had diabetes, and Jamila couldn't get him to stay on his medication. Jamila, who cared about Ben as a patient and even saw a bit of herself in him (they were both musicians), grew tremendously frustrated as she watched Ben suffer health consequences from his inconsistent approach to his own care. Jamila left the last appointment feeling depleted and angry. She knew she had shown her frustration more than was optimal, and that she needed to cool off and figure out another approach.

When Jamila took a moment to contemplate a prior success in her work with this patient, she realized that, in fact, she had been successful with this patient a few times before. When Ben had first come to Jamila for treatment, for example, he had been struggling with very poor eating habits. Jamila had spent time talking to Ben, asking him questions about his life and what made him happy. Most important, Jamila reassured him that change could feel manageable. Ben had agreed to see a nutritionist and overall was eating better than when he first came in. He had even lost a bit of weight. Jamila realized that her negotiation with this longtime patient was not an overall failure, and that maybe the medication issue posed more of a speed bump than a roadblock.

Placing the negotiation into context by considering a prior success also works wonders for difficult negotiations where you don't have a long-term relationship with the other person. I also spoke to an advertising executive, Elijah, about a recent failed negotiation; he had interviewed for a job he really wanted, and then tried to come to terms with company management about compensation and job responsibilities. They resisted some of the terms Elijah felt were non-negotiable. Eventually, the back-and-forth generated a lot of bad feelings on both sides. They mutually agreed Elijah would not take the job.

Elijah was very upset about the way things had gone down. He went back and forth between anger at how they had handled things and self-doubt about his approach. Frustrated and sad, he stopped his job-seeking efforts for a little while. But when Elijah prompted himself to consider his prior successes in job negotiation, he realized that over the course of his career he had successfully negotiated his way into almost a dozen jobs—some that he took, and some where he liked the offer but ultimately made another choice. By placing this recent "failure" into context, Elijah realized that one bad job negotiation did not define his worth as a negotiator, or in the market. He restarted his search.

Like Jamila or Elijah, you might find some of those negative feelings melting away as you consider how you handled a similar situation successfully and place this negotiation in its proper context. Once we take the time to remind ourselves of a prior success, we reduce the noise in our minds and allow ourselves to see that this negotiation is just one of many we have tackled in our lifetime.

Your Prior Success as a Data Generator

The second benefit of this question is that it acts as a data generator, helping you to recall strategies that have worked in the past and might work for you again. Andrew, the executive whose story started this chapter, considered a prior success (or two) and generated a helpful action list of things to try in his compensation negotiation. He left with an action plan that included research, argument formulation, meeting with key players, and self-motivation.

I've seen this work over and over again for other people in vastly different situations.

Smith is a contractor who has done many jobs for Rosa, a landlord and business owner. After many years of working together happily and profitably on many of Rosa's apartments, their last job, a kitchen renovation, ended with a breached agreement, no payment, an unfinished kitchen, and a lot of bad feelings. They were left trying to negotiate how much money would be paid, and whether or how they would work together going forward. As their mediator, I asked them how they had handled their dealings successfully in the past. Several important things happened almost immediately. First, they remembered just how many projects they had completed together over the years with absolutely no issue. This helped place their current dispute into context and focus them on the fact that the relationship had been mostly good. Second, they were able to diagnose that certain practices that had worked for them in the past—writing out the contract, picking out fixtures together—were missing from this last deal, which had been rushed and more involved than their typical projects. After focusing on these previous successes, we restored some of the good feeling between them and gave them ideas for the future. They decided to continue to work together and to always create a written contract. And they set some guidelines for ways they would communicate about design choices once a job was in progress.

Brad is a father of a tween girl, Harper, who struggles with anxiety that manifests in explosive arguments at home. These "blowouts," as Brad calls them, usually occur when Harper is heading off to school in the morning. They have affected the whole family, including Brad's other two children and spouse, and lately have driven Brad to the point of yelling himself, which makes him feel terrible. Brad has been trying desperately to negotiate this situation with Harper, but has started to despair about his ability to make it better.

When I asked Brad about a prior success, it took him a few minutes to get into the headspace to consider it. Once he did, though, he thought of one: years earlier, Harper had a difficult time mastering reading. She struggled with confidence and fought Brad every night over homework. They had a number of similar "high volume" arguments that ended in tears on both sides. Eventually, Brad helped her over the hump. How? In looking back, Brad realized that he had done a couple of things. One, he had found Harper a reading tutor who was young, and who Harper looked up to and respected. The tutor had made a personal connection with Harper and that translated into more motivation to read. Second, Brad had made an effort to spend more one-on-one time with Harper when they weren't reading. They did activities they both enjoyed, like going to kids' museums or out for ice cream. Brad felt this had helped them build their relationship so that they could get through the difficult times around Harper's reading.

With this information, Brad decided to look for a young, personable therapist who might be able to connect with Harper and help with her anxiety. He also made a commitment to spending a couple hours a week with Harper at a less stressful time, to connect and do things they both enjoyed. He started to feel more optimistic about his ability to help Harper—and himself—get through this latest challenge.

In both of these situations, looking at a prior success helped someone approach a challenging negotiation with some concrete ideas that gave them a roadmap toward continued success. If this applies to you, take a moment to see if your prior success helps you generate ideas for your own negotiation.

Priming Yourself for Creativity and Success in Negotiation

There's one additional, powerful benefit to considering a prior success as part of your negotiation strategy. When you consider a prior success, you feel better. And when you feel better, you increase the chances that you will perform better in your next negotiation. One of the main reasons to ask this question is that, in addition to placing your situation in context and generating helpful ideas, it makes you feel empowered, happy, and proud in a way that has a positive impact on the issue you are working on.

We also know from chapter 3, and many studies, that focusing on positive events may increase your creativity and resourcefulness in negotiation. One study at Columbia found that graduate business school candidates who wrote about an experience of personal power prior to participating in a mock job interview saw their odds of acceptance shoot up: They were accepted 68 percent of the time, compared with a normal acceptance rate of 47 percent. And people who wrote about a time in which they lacked power plummeted in effectiveness, with only 26 percent of them getting selected by the judges.

And in another recent study, researchers at Harvard Business School found a close link between positive emotion and creativity that proved to be very helpful in negotiation, especially when the negotiating parties reached moments of difficulty. As researchers Teresa Amabile and Steven Kramer explained in their subsequent book *The Progress Principle*, this effect is self-reinforcing. Says the *Harvard Business Review* of their work: "Positive feelings increase creativity, which in turn can lead to positive feelings within a team or an organization. Creativity is particularly important in negotiation when the parties are at an impasse."

The process of negotiating, not to mention the substantive issues that we're negotiating about, can lead us to feel anxious or disempowered as we prepare for our next negotiation. Generating positive feelings around a prior negotiation success may be just what we need to carry that positive emotion forward and access the creativity and decision-making capabilities that will make us successful in our next negotiation.

Tip for Recalling a Prior Success

We know all the benefits you can experience when you contemplate a prior success. Now I have a tip for you when you are answering this question. This is important, so don't skip it! When you consider "How have I successfully handled this in the past?" I want you to do something before you write your answer down. I want you to close your eyes and picture it—your previous triumph—in as much detail as possible. Go ahead and play some Rocky-style montage music in your head (or out loud!) as you do it. What did it feel like? Sound like? Taste like? What posture were you in? What location? What outfit? Visualize yourself making your pitch as the client nods. Experience the relief as your spouse says, "I get it," feel the joy of the handshake as you make a deal—or as the money hits your bank account.

I also want you to remember the time leading up to that moment. Picture your preparation. Your thoughts. Your tasks. Your emotion. All of this is data—remembering everything that went into your prior success can help you prepare to repeat it. Remember, when you recall a previous success, you are more likely to perform better in your next negotiation. The more you can picture it, the more you'll put yourself back in that mind frame to achieve another triumph.

Your Turn in the Mirror

Now it's your turn to look in the Mirror. Remember, you've already identified your needs and what's brought you here. You've considered your feelings, positive and otherwise. Now you're going to look at a prior success. As you did in the other chapters, create the occasion by finding a physical space where you can think and write freely, and allow yourself to consider this question: *How have I handled this successfully in the past?*

Write as much as you can for the next five minutes.

Troubleshooting

Now let's tackle a couple of issues that might come up when you're considering a prior success.

1. "I don't have a similar success"

So, what if you can't recall a similar success? Again, like Andrew did at the beginning of this chapter, you'll want to break down this negotiation to think about the steps this situation involves, and what you might need to be successful. (Verbs tend to be especially helpful here: researching, framing, psyching up, for example.)

I did this exercise with a group of business graduate students in Brazil. One student, Frida, a businesswoman who was returning to school to further her career, and who had participated in the first day of my course with a lot of confidence, gave me an apprehensive look when I told the class we would be working through the questions in this book to help them with an upcoming negotiation. At first, she approached me privately to ask, "So . . . let's say you're working through a career change. Does that count as a negotiation?" I said, "Absolutely. You're steering your career toward your goals. These steering conversations are negotiations." She looked more resigned than happy to hear this situation counted for the exercise.

I saw her work through her problem definition, her needs, and even her emotions. She continued to look apprehensive, but gamely wrote down her answers. Then we got to this question, about a prior success. This was when she openly teared up and put her head in her hands. I walked over so we could speak privately. She took a deep breath and exhaled forcefully: "This is the situation. I was fired from my last job. Fired! I mean, I knew it wasn't working. Honestly, I hated the work I was doing—that's the reason I applied to graduate school. I thought I'd have time to make my next plan. But it ended before I was totally ready. I need to accept that this happened and figure out a new direction. But I don't have a prior success at this. That's the whole reason this is so bad. I've never been fired before!"

We worked together to summarize her answer. She needed to (1) accept that this work relationship, which was not satisfying or successful from her point of view but was serving a purpose at the time, had ended, and (2) figure out a new, more satisfying direction for herself. I asked her, "Can you recall a prior time when you succeeded in accepting the end of a chapter and crafting a new beginning for yourself?" For a few seconds she shook her head and sat in silence. Then she looked up. "Wait—yes. Would a personal relationship count? I had a long-term relationship that just wasn't working, for either of us. There were some good aspects, and the companionship was nice, but I knew that we just weren't meant to be.

So we ended it. I was sad, but after a few days I was also excited for the future. I knew that now I had freed myself up to be with someone who would be my 'forever.' I started plugging back into my hobbies and starting conversations with people that I thought might share interests with me that would make us more compatible for the long term."

This brief conversation helped Frida greatly. Contemplating a prior success in starting a new chapter after the end of a relationship took some of the sting out of the experience of being fired. She was able to remind herself that the work relationship, like her prior personal relationship, was mutually unsatisfying. And she remembered that she had, in fact, achieved success in designing a new chapter of her life. She decided to get involved with some professional associations that aligned with her interests (similar to the way she had rediscovered her hobbies after her breakup). And she was able to recognize that even her graduate school acceptance, and the networking possibilities it presented, was a major step toward designing that better future for herself. She stood a bit taller as she walked out the door that day.

2. "I can't think of a success at all"

Occasionally, I get someone who tells me they can't think of a success. At all. Sometimes people, no matter how successful or accomplished they appear to be from the outside, have difficulty describing their own work as successful. They may attribute the outcome to other people ("It was a team effort") or luck ("I was in the right place at the right time"). For others, their standard for what counts as a success is so high as to exclude . . . well, everything (e.g., "I submitted my op-ed to multiple major newspapers. One of them snapped it up right away, but cut it down significantly to be printed as a letter."). And still others, including Michelle Obama and Sheryl Sandberg, have described suffering from a well-known phenomenon called "impostor syndrome," in which instead of considering yourself a success, you're just waiting for the world to recognize you for the fraud you know you are.

Sound familiar? Whether you're dealing with a confidence gap or imposter syndrome, you might run into difficulty when you're trying to recall a prior success in order to feel more confident and competent in your negotiations. Awareness is the first step. Sometimes just by knowing these phenomena exist, we can recognize them in our lives and start to unpack their effects.

First, let me emphasize that your prior success doesn't have to be something huge, like landing the deal that transformed your company and ended up leading to an initial public offering. Take some time to think about a period when things went well at/with work or in your personal life. A time you felt proud, even in the moment. Or when you received a piece of positive feedback. Maybe that's your prior success.

And speaking of feedback, my second tip is to try consulting a friend or close colleague—either for real, or in your imagination. What would your closest colleague on the team say about your contribution to that team project? What would your best friend say you excel at? Sometimes, feedback from a close, respected person in your life can be enough to help shake loose a prior success. I did this exercise with a friend who was looking for a new job after significant time off as a stay-at-home parent, and found himself struggling with self-confidence about his ability to interview his way back into the workforce. He told me that when he tried to identify a prior success, he drew a blank. "That's the issue. Basically, I haven't had a real job outside the home since right after college. I'm a completely different person now." I asked him, "What about your at-home job? What are the things you're best at or that bring you the most satisfaction?" He said, "Well, I pay all the bills and I'm always on time. My partner did that for a while, but I'm much better at it. So I took it over. And when our son was diagnosed with dyslexia, I coordinated all the testing. I advocated with his school to make sure they supported him in the classroom as required by law. And I found a tutor that I knew would be a good match for his needs." In other words, my "unsuccessful" friend was a very organized manager who could handle multiple deadlines at once. He could research legal standards, make successful arguments, and coordinate policy implementation. Hearing all this from a good friend allowed him to see his prior success, and how that could translate into his negotiation efforts to land a full-time job.

Sometimes, your prior success will contain lots of clues to help you negotiate better in the present and future. But even if the success is quite different from the challenge in front of you, just knowing that you have been successful at your prior endeavors will help put emotional gas in your tank to go forth and negotiate.

Wrapping Up

With this question answered, you've almost finished looking in the Mirror. In this chapter, you identified a time when you handled a similar negotiation challenge successfully. If you didn't have an obviously similar prior success, you searched your internal data bank for any successes that share some common elements with the negotiation facing you now. And you may have worked through some mental baggage in actually recognizing prior events or your personal qualities as a success. Before we finish, take a moment to read through what you wrote down for this chapter, and summarize any important points or themes.

Next, we'll move on to a question with which we consider the future, and get you started on designing it.

FIVE

WHAT'S THE FIRST STEP?

Mei Xu walked into Bloomingdale's in New York City, taking a moment to contemplate the sights, sounds, and scents. Years ago, she had walked through these doors as a customer. Today, she was an entrepreneur.

Mei emigrated from China to the U.S. in 1991, after working at the World Bank and training for a career as a Chinese diplomat. Thanks to her diplomatic education, which included not only English language lessons but also courses in Renaissance art—and hours spent browsing the clothing stalls that sprang up next to her middle school—she arrived in the U.S. deeply interested in art and fashion. But she didn't have any relevant experience in that field, and she needed a job to support herself. So she took a position working for an American medical device company that exported equipment to Chinese hospitals. The work was boring, but it paid the bills.

Fortuitously, her company housed her in a New York City hotel next to the department store Bloomingdale's. On her off-hours, she would find herself walking around Bloomingdale's, looking longingly at the wares for sale. She was amazed at the incredible sense of fashion she saw in their women's clothing, but when she walked into the home department, she saw something very different. The sense of fashion that permeated the rest of Bloomingdale's was totally lacking in home furnishings—most of which looked to Mei like they were stuck decades in the past, like "Grandma's wallpaper." Mei told Guy Raz of NPR that her goal was to "close the gap between home and fashion."

Her first step was to negotiate where in home goods she could best make her mark. After evaluating various business possibilities, she decided to focus on scented candles. She did some research and took a guess that with the right upscale look and scent, people would buy those candles not just at holiday time but year-round.

But first, she needed to figure out how to make one.

So her next step was to gain experience by trial and error. She went to a fragrance vendor in New Jersey to learn how to blend scents with wax. And then she spent weeks making trial candles in her basement, using Campbell's Soup cans as molds and experimenting with adding scents. One day during her experiments, she forgot to add a chemical that made the oil blend with the wax. So when she took the candle out of the mold, it looked different—fossilized, or aged—due to the lack of this chemical. Mei decided to make this mistake part of her candle's brand, which she launched in 1994: the Chesapeake Bay Candle Company.

Her next step was to negotiate her way into stores. Mei told me, "Taking things one step at a time is very important. I sold my candles in mom-and-pop stores because I knew that in order to survive against the big chains, they had to know the trends really, really well. I knew I would benefit from what I learned there, and that it would help me take the next step to the big stores when we were ready."

Armed with her local success, Mei went to Bloomingdale's, where she started by building relationships with the assistants who answered the phones. Every time she called or visited, she would ask them about themselves: where they lived before this job, what made them want to work in fashion. Eventually, using charm and persistence, she got them to give her the name of the buyer, the person who made decisions about what products Bloomingdale's would order. The buyer immediately loved Mei's candles and placed an order to sell them—in the same Bloomingdale's stores where Mei had built her relationships.

As soon as she landed this life-changing order, the next step became apparent to Mei. She needed to fulfill it. Fulfilling the order would require a dedicated facility to produce her unique candles, including the fragrance oil she would need. Mei called her sister, who was working together with Mei's brother-in-law at a computer company in Hangzhou, China. Hearing what she needed, they mobilized, and in 1995, opened a factory to make the candles. The factory is still in operation today.

After her Bloomingdale's success, Mei knew where she needed to go next to grow the company. In order to reach a larger segment of the market, she would need to get into a store that presented more options for value-focused consumers, but which also had a reputation for good design. She set her sights on Target, which had 750 stores nationally and two dedicated aisles with forty-eight feet of candle space.

However, the persistence and relationship-building techniques that got her into Bloomingdale's fell flat at Target. Despite an entire year of outreach, Mei couldn't get the buyer to return her calls. Finally, the sympathetic receptionist suggested Mei call the buyer's boss and complain. She did. The buyer called her back immediately—only to yell at her that this was not the way to start a relationship, before hanging up.

Deflated, Mei waited a bit, but then she called again. And again. And finally, months later, a different voice greeted her on the voice mail. Mei received a quick call back from the new, very young buyer, and flew to Target headquarters in Minneapolis to meet with her. The buyer ended the meeting by saying, "Mei, I want to put your candles in all 750 of our stores." Target placed an order worth over $1 million, with a forecast for the year of more than $3 million.

Mei's series of candle experiments, conducted in the basement of her home using Campbell's Soup cans, eventually led to the creation of her multimillion-dollar company Chesapeake Bay Candle. In a little more than twenty years, Mei went from landing on U.S. soil knowing no one but her husband, and with no design or consumer goods experience, to building a huge company that would later sell to Newell Brands, a multibillion-dollar consumer goods company, for a reported $75 million dollars.

And she did it one step at a time.

What's the First Step?

To end our Mirror session, I want to ask you about the future. We started by defining our problem or goal and examining what led to it. Then, we explored our needs and feelings, which helped set our priorities and make decisions. After, we generated momentum and ideas by investigating a prior success. Now it's time to take the first step—it's time to start designing the future.

I often work with people who have correctly identified the problem they need to solve but haven't yet figured out how to fix it completely. In this chapter, we'll investigate the reason why focusing on your first step is so effective for negotiation success. After we explore the *why* of this question, we turn to the *how*: I will help you focus your attention on yourself, tap into your inner wisdom, and plot your first steps forward.

Taking That First Step Forward

I like to say that every negotiation involves time travel: we need to understand the past and the present before we move to designing a better future. In this chapter, we are looking to the future. This is the last phase of our time in the Mirror.

Asking yourself "What's the first step?" is important for two main reasons: it builds momentum and enables the next steps.

One Step at a Time Builds Momentum

First, focusing on the first step can help us build momentum. When facing a negotiation or steering ourselves toward a big and exciting goal, trying to design the whole solution from the outset can feel more overwhelming than productive. And being overwhelmed can lead even the most motivated people to give up prematurely or approach things in a haphazard way. Sometimes, we need that one step to help us build a little momentum.

When I coach a team through a negotiation where we have multiple issues on the table, I like to have them list everything on a whiteboard for all of us to see. Then I pick one issue to start with—one where I know we are likely to have success. And once we cross that off the board, you can see the looks of relief around the room and feel the excitement start to build. We're on our way. And that helps everyone stay motivated to start solving the rest of the issues before us.

I recently spoke to a well-known journalist at the top of her game, who has covered prominent stories all over broadcast media, but who privately has been beating herself up for several years over the one major career step she has yet to accomplish: writing a book. She told me, "I think my main talent is that I can synthesize large amounts of research quickly and digest it for people in an easy-to-understand format. I'm used to getting the idea for a story at three p.m. and then appearing on the news an hour or two later. This past year in particular, I've been covering some of the biggest stories out there. One of these could be sold as a book proposal pretty quickly if I got the story just right. I just need to figure out how to do this while also doing my reporting job."

At this point, she was ready to look forward. I asked her, "What's one step you could take right now, in your spare time, to get yourself ready so that when that one big story hits, you could quickly transfer your material into a proposal and shop it?"

She thought about it. "Wow. You know, I could start by writing the non-time-sensitive parts of a book proposal—like my autobiographical information and a market analysis—so that when I know I have *that story*, the one that's going to be my book, I could just drop it in and send it out. This way I've set myself up for the thing I do best—get a story, and get it quickly—to help me land a deal. I'm going to do that this week!" Two months later, she's nearly finished her book proposal. Sometimes, focusing on the first step helps us organize our thoughts and take back our own power.

One Step as Preparation for the Next

The second reason to start with the first step is that many times negotiation is cumulative. We can't take the fifth step, for example, until we have traveled the first four. Mei Xu told me that one of the biggest mistakes entrepreneurs make is skipping steps in their negotiations. She knew she needed experience selling her candles in smaller venues before she would amass the experience, judgment, and proof of sales needed to take her company to the next level with a larger buyer.

The same is true for the book you're reading right now! In order to figure out the best first step for you to take, you need to do the work of figuring out where you want to go, what you need, what you're feeling, and how you have been successful in the past. Answering all these questions prepares you to answer this final question and help you solve your issue.

One Step at a Time: Some Examples

Considering the first step can be transformative, no matter what kind of negotiation you are facing. Sometimes the first step can feel small but carry a huge impact. One United Nations ambassador, Luis Gallegos of Ecuador, told me that in major diplomatic negotiations, where you have dozens, if not hundreds, of players, people can sway the final vote by changing one word in a massive document. One small business owner, Julie, wanted to start attracting bigger work, and so after landing one large client, she decided to start documenting her work for that client on social media, so that people could see her capability. That one decision landed her multiple new large clients.

Taking things one step at a time is especially useful when you're steering yourself toward a large goal.

Celebrity trainer Autumn Calabrese has helped many people achieve health- and fitness-related goals and lose large amounts of weight. Autumn told me that she sees losing weight as—you guessed it—a negotiation, and one that is common to a lot of people around the world. She recently built a nutrition program that focuses on having people ask themselves questions, in order to take a deeper look in the Mirror and start steering themselves toward their goals.

Autumn told me, "I try to get my clients to ask themselves the deeper questions that can help lead them to the real answers about their issue, as well as real solutions. Most people are on that hamster wheel of jumping from diet to diet. When you do that, you're never stopping to ask yourself the deeper, harder questions about what's going on for you.

"And once we have those answers, setting short-term goals [is] the first step. So if your long-term goal is, 'I want to lose fifty pounds,' great. We need a roadmap to get there. We can't just say, 'I want to lose fifty pounds,' and then wing it. I have people start with small steps, maybe one per week. So we say, 'Okay, what do we need to do in week one, week two, week three, and week four?' Those are small steps, and we take them one at a time. We do this for a couple of reasons. One, those individual steps help motivate people. You need little celebrations along the way, because fifty pounds is a big number—it's not going to happen overnight, so we need small victories to happen along the way to keep us going.

"The second reason to do things step-by-step is that you need each step to progress. If you're trying to lose fifty pounds, you may not be able to add in a lot of exercise, for example, until you're eating well and giving yourself more energy. So maybe in week 1 you say, 'I'm going to drink less soda,' and then week 2 is eating more vegetables, and then, once you're feeling better, the step for week 3 is walking a couple of times a week. So you have those small steps along the way that add up to the big goal. At the beginning, I think it is really important to just focus on step one. You don't have to know all the steps yet. You don't have to know where you need to be at month 6. So let's talk about what we can do in weeks 1 and 2 to start getting closer to that goal. That first week is all about us talking and asking, 'What's step one?'"

Your Turn in the Mirror

Now it's your turn to look in the Mirror. Remember, you've already identified what's brought you here, and your needs. You've considered your feelings, positive and otherwise. You've examined a prior success. And now you're going to look to the future. As you did in the other chapters, create the occasion to answer this question in a comfortable space where you can think and write freely. Allow yourself to consider this question:

What's the first step?

Wrapping Up the Mirror Section: Designing Your Steps Forward

In this chapter, we will wrap up our work looking in the Mirror. You've just written down one or more "first steps" you can take in your negotiation as a roadmap for the future. Now we're going to make that roadmap as complete as possible. Together, we will take your history from chapter 1, your needs from chapter 2, feelings from chapter 3, successes from chapter 4, and then use them to design your next steps in this chapter—putting them together in an action plan that leaves you feeling confident, empowered, and connected to yourself and your goals.

Reviewing Your Problem (or Goal)

First, I want you to take a look back at your summary for chapter 1. What was the problem or goal you identified? Again, all of our decisions in negotiation flow from the reason we're here. If, like Steve Jobs, you are designing a mini-computer that people can use for every purpose, which also makes phone calls, you're studying all the separate devices that people currently carry, and figuring out how to build those functions into your device. If you're negotiating with your contractor to build your dream bathroom, you're researching the latest design innovations and which of those you want in your home; if, instead, you're fixing up your home to sell it, you're figuring out what someone else wants—you're looking at the bathrooms from the last few homes that sold in your neighborhood and making sure your design compares to theirs.

You'll also want to take a look at any history that led you to where you are today. If you're Antonia working through a major dispute with your sister Carmen, or Andrew gathering data for his compensation negotiation, you want to go back through the brief history of your issue and consider what's happened to date when thinking about the best steps forward.

Looking Back at Your Needs

Next, I want you to focus back on the needs you uncovered in chapter 2. Remember that you looked at both tangibles (what you can count, see, or touch) and intangibles (the themes or values, like appreciation and respect, that give our lives meaning). These are what's most important to you, and any steps you take should reflect those needs.

When you consider your intangibles, go back to the follow-up question I asked, to explore any specific ideas that came up under "What would that look like?" Remember that something like fairness will look vastly different to different people. For one person, it might be a $20,000 addition to her base salary. For another, it's going to look like better placement for his art in the gallery exhibition. For yet another, it's going to be that each spouse takes a night cleaning the kitchen. Take a look back now at the specific items that brought your intangibles to life.

And then, reviewing all your needs, think about what actions you could take to *fully and completely* meet those needs. Remember, successful aspirations in negotiation are based on our needs, so be specific as well as optimistic. Give yourself permission to consider a world in which all your needs could be met, and then make a list of concrete first steps to get there. If you're finding this hard, pretend I'm handing you a twenty-dollar bill for every idea you generate. Crazy, impractical—it doesn't matter. Some of the world's successful negotiations have come from an improbable-sounding first idea.

Consider a now-famous negotiation success story from Teddy Roosevelt's presidential campaign in 1912. Toward the end of the campaign, Roosevelt and his campaign manager planned for a whistle-stop trip by train, one in which Roosevelt expected to meet millions of potential voters. They had printed three million copies of a pamphlet that contained one of Roosevelt's speeches along with a flattering picture. Shortly before they left, however, the campaign realized they had a serious problem: they had not secured permission from Moffett Studios, the copyright holder of the picture. In researching the law, they discovered that if they went ahead and distributed the pamphlets without the copyright, they could be liable for one dollar per picture. They couldn't afford the risk. They needed an idea, fast.

Roosevelt's campaign manager, George Perkins, came up with one. But it sounded improbable. He sent Moffett Studios the following cable:

"We are planning to distribute millions of pamphlets with Roosevelt's picture on the cover. It will be great publicity for the studio whose photograph we use. How much will you pay us to use yours? Respond immediately."

Moffett replied to the cable and said that although he'd never done something like this before, he'd be willing to offer them $250. They accepted. Roosevelt's campaign turned a potential liability into a financial benefit. All they needed was one good idea.

Looking at Your Feelings

After considering your problem and your needs, look back at what you wrote about your feelings in chapter 3. Feelings—positive and negative— are part of any negotiation, and they can help us make decisions.

Recognizing your feelings may help you to craft better solutions. Recall the magic follow-up question that helps anyone turn feelings into future-focused ideas. If you are feeling any negative emotions, ask yourself: "What would help eliminate or reduce my [insert negative feeling] in this situation?" Recall the example of a doctor, Jamila, who is negotiating how to care for a certain patient, and who discovers that her overwhelming emotion is frustration. In this situation, Jamila may ask herself, "What would help eliminate or reduce my frustration in this situation?" When you ask this follow-up question, you start to use your feelings as an idea generator to give you concrete ideas for how to move forward. If you didn't do this in chapter 3, take a moment to look now and see what steps would help you decrease these negative emotions. (And, by the way, you can do the opposite with your positive emotions. If you're feeling joy at the way certain aspects of your career have progressed, try asking yourself, "What steps could I take to maintain or increase my joy?")

Considering a Prior Success

Finally, go back to your answers from chapter 4 about a prior success, whether it was similar to the problem you're facing now, or a success in a different arena. What did you envision when you closed your eyes and recalled everything in detail—your habits, actions, mental state—that led to that negotiation success? If you have a similar prior success, take a look at that again now and see what steps you took there that might work again here. For example, if you're negotiating with your spouse on your different attitudes toward money, and this was something that worked well in the early years of your marriage, you might look back at the past and see what made you two successful at handling this issue back then. This not only helps you feel better about your current situation, but gives you useful data on what might work. You also can use this prior success when you talk to the other person in this negotiation, as evidence of an approach you know has worked.

And if you don't have a similar prior success, take a look at the unrelated prior success you listed in chapter 4. If you're negotiating your salary for the first time and that makes you anxious, but you realized in chapter 4 that you are excellent at making client pitches and convincing people of the strength of your ideas, you can examine what leads you to that success (and confidence) and see what steps you can replicate for this negotiation.

What If I Came Up with a Lot More Than One Step?

You've just reviewed all the work you did in the first four chapters of this book and come up with some ideas for how to move forward. Great! If you did some writing in the first five minutes you set aside for this chapter, and you're still coming up with ideas, write them all down now.

As you're reading this chapter, and even afterward, feel free to write down as many ideas as come to mind. By asking you to come up with one step, I don't mean to limit you if the ideas are flowing. The idea behind taking one step is to free you from feeling as though you have to know all the answers now. Because most of the time, you won't. Sometimes, even if we have a lot of ideas now, we need the other person we'll be negotiating with in order to figure out potential solutions (we'll get to that in the upcoming Window section). And sometimes, the road we're on is too long to see the final destination. We can feel stymied trying to solve it all in one go. But even if you're not able to design your entire future just yet, you likely have a sense of what you want your tomorrow to look like. So instead of trying to see all the turns you'll need to make on your GPS, let's just focus on the one that's next.

Troubleshooting

Occasionally when I ask people this question, they have trouble coming up with an answer. Let's troubleshoot a couple of reasons you might experience a speed bump when answering this question.

Too Many Cooks in the Kitchen

As we've talked about in prior chapters, one of the main reasons people have trouble thinking of steps forward is that they're hearing other voices in their head. In other words, your older sister, outspoken coworker, or your close friends or family members have already weighed in and given you advice—asked or unasked. Perhaps they've gone beyond advice and even *told* you what you should do about your negotiation.

I see this sometimes when I teach negotiation. When I assign all the students in my class to negotiate a particular problem—let's say a negotiation over the price for a used car—and have people meet in groups, buyer and seller, to discuss their answers to the Mirror questions, occasionally you can see on someone's face that they are beginning to second-guess themselves after hearing someone else's priorities. Should I be pushing for a payment plan, like this other person wants? Demand a third-party inspection by a person I alone can choose? Suddenly, their own list of needs feels less legitimate next to someone else's.

And if this happens during a role play in class—which is just a simulation—imagine how much we might allow someone's advice to sway us in real life, when the stakes can be high. So what do you do if you're drawing a blank, or if you're feeling conflicted as you're writing answers to this question? Consider whether you might be hearing what someone else thinks is your first step forward. Has anyone talked with you about the negotiation you are working on? Engage with those voices in your head by asking yourself: Who are the different audiences to your issue—maybe your coworkers, clients, spouse, kids—and then ask yourself, What would they think is your first step? Write it down. Then study it. What seems right to you about what you wrote? What doesn't resonate? This will help you develop your own critique of other people's ideas for you, so that you can develop your own sense of what will work for you. Eventually, your goal will be to move other people's perspectives to the side so that you can tune in to your own goals and design your own steps forward.

"I'm Stuck"

What if you've read this chapter and still can't think of anything in answer to this question? Read on.

SET THE OCCASION, AGAIN. I want you to think once again about setting the occasion for this question. I want you to go beyond setting aside time in your day to think about *where* and *when* you do your best idea generation. Morning, noon, or night? At work, or at home? During a long run? In a busy coffeehouse? Or a quiet library? Wherever you're most likely to generate creative ideas, that's where you want to think about this question.

ASKING YOURSELF THE WORST OPTION. If you're still feeling stuck or inhibited, let's play a game. Ask yourself the following question: "What's the *worst* step I could take?" Sometimes, we are self-censoring what we really want. Or we need the freedom to try on a bunch of options before we figure out what works. Freeing ourselves to consider the worst-case scenario often gives us clarity on what might be better.

One manufacturing executive needed to decide whether to accept a promotion within his current department, where he had mastered all the job functions and had been very successful but couldn't stand the workplace climate, or to transfer to a totally new international division where he didn't know anyone and would have to get up to speed on 50 percent of the job responsibilities. He was scheduled to sit down with the two departments within a week to negotiate. When I asked him to come up with his first step, he answered, "I'm not sure. I've been going back and forth about the future of the company and what division will offer the best path forward for me. I've already gotten all the information I think I can from each of these departments." So I asked him, "What's the worst step you could take at this point?" He closed his eyes, paused a moment, and then surprised himself by answering, "I can't stay here another year. I don't have a good feeling about where my department is going. It's time." He accepted the offer to move to the new international division. Considering the "worst" option freed his mind up and gave him clarity that he needed to make a decision.

This "worst idea" method works well for individuals, and just as well (or better) for negotiations that involve a group. In fact, some companies use this technique to help them generate innovative business ideas. 3M calls this "reverse thinking," or "turning the problem upside down." As an example, when pondering the issue of how to get more customers to subscribe to their newsletter, they might ask, "How can we get people to unsubscribe to our newsletter?" If answering that question ends up generating steps like, "Include content that isn't relevant to consumers' lives," "Mail people too often," or "Don't include promotions or discounts for products we know will interest them" . . . well, you can already start to see what your first several steps toward the solution might be. If you started this chapter having issues with thinking of even one step forward, try thinking of the worst step, and see what ideas come to mind. You might surprise yourself.

Wrapping Up

Congratulations! You've completed the Mirror section of this book. By asking yourself these five questions and listening closely to your answers, you've started your negotiation way ahead of where you were before—and where most people begin. You've uncovered a lot of information that gives you deep insight into yourself and your issue, as well as lots of ideas for potential solutions. Take one last look over your answers and summarize any last thoughts on what you've discovered.

Now, we move on to the Window. For some people, looking in the Mirror and talking to themselves feels more challenging than sitting down with someone else. And for the rest of you . . . you might be thinking, *Do I really need to do this with someone else?*

First of all, that's a closed question, so I'm going to reframe it: Go ahead and ask yourself, "What do I have to gain by asking questions of someone else?" This is a much better question. Why? Because of course you don't *have* to do anything. You could take what I call the ostrich approach to negotiation—sticking your head in the sand and waiting until the issue goes away. But you stand to gain a lot by taking the plunge. When I tell people to ask for more and teach them how to get it, this—a clear window into someone else—is a huge part of the *more* this approach to negotiation offers you. What is that *more* again?

- More options for a valuable solution
- More confidence that you can talk to anyone, or handle any issue that comes your way
- More progress toward your personal goals, by understanding the people who may be important to your success
- More closeness with another person
- By asking someone else questions that expand the pie of information available to you, more of a head start toward your next negotiation
- More peace of mind that comes with honest (and compassionate) conversation

But don't worry, you won't be doing this alone. Just as I did for the Mirror section of this book, I will guide you as you complete the Window questions. I will give you an overview of how to ask each question and listen for the answers so that you get as much as possible from the conversation. I will give you some insight into what may happen when you ask each question. I'll give you tips on how to follow up and troubleshoot any difficulties. And then I will help you use the information you gather from the Window questions to move forward toward your solution.

PART 2

THE WINDOW

When people talk, listen completely. Most people never listen.
—ERNEST HEMINGWAY

Research, and our own experiences, show how hard it can be to truly see another person. The same film clouding the mirror and preventing us from seeing ourselves is also fogging up the window we should be using to see the person next to us.

Even in ordinary circumstances we have trouble seeing people clearly, without the "noise" of our own experiences, judgments, and emotions. Hearing, sight, and touch can fail to deliver an accurate perception. And it's even more challenging when we engage in negotiation or try to make a deal. We often fail to hear—or worse, actively devalue—what comes out of another person's mouth during a challenging conversation. And when we do ask questions, we often ask closed questions, which shut down communication and may influence the other person to give answers they think you want to hear, rather than what they actually want to say.

The Window section of this book is about raising the right questions and then listening to the answers. And in order to listen—really listen—to another person, we need to hear their needs, concerns, and feelings, not just prepare our response.

People sometimes tell me they don't need to ask any questions when negotiating because they "have the information already," or "have heard it all a million times." Not once have I found that to be true. Even with people we feel like we've known forever, we are less than perfect listeners, especially when it comes to the important stuff. We tune out, we get distracted, or we hear things through the static of our own perceptions.

Funny enough, I've found that of all the people I teach every year—diplomats, lawyers, executives, human resources professionals—the best listeners are the ten-year-old girls I teach about conflict resolution in my New Jersey hometown. Why do these girls outperform us adults in listening? They're not thinking about themselves, while we allow our own needs and feelings to cloud our view of the people around us. This section will help you clear up your window to hear, and see, the person sitting across from you better. And when you hear better, you steer better.

Listening to an Adversary?

Most people understand the importance of listening to a spouse, colleague, or someone with whom they're having an important conversation. But perhaps you're skeptical about listening to someone you're going up against in a fierce negotiation, thinking the same techniques might not apply under these circumstances.

They do. Even if you are in a true win-lose negotiation, where usually only one person can win, spending time listening to and observing your opponent will give you the greatest chance of success. It works the same way in sports. Take tennis as an example: observing the angle of the other player's racket and his footwork, as well as listening to the sound his shot makes, will tell you whether to expect a hard shot down the line or a softer slice. You're then better positioned to hit your own shot.

The same is true of monetary negotiations. Rather than stating your desired monetary amount or position up front, starting your negotiation by asking questions about the other person's needs, concerns, and goals gives you the best chance of pitching your proposal with success and creating value from a seemingly win-lose situation. Professor Leigh Thompson at the Kellogg School of Management found that 93 percent of all negotiators failed to ask diagnostic questions about their counterpart's needs, concerns, and goals in circumstances where getting them answered would have significantly improved their outcomes. So even if you're at odds, listening to the other side will help you in negotiation.

Remember, many times your adversary at the table becomes (or stays) your partner once the deal is done. That contractor you're negotiating with on your bathroom? Once you've settled on a price, you're trusting her to build a room you'll love for years to come. If you're a product company negotiating with a distributor, once you've settled on price and terms, you need them to be a committed, enthusiastic partner in getting your product into as many homes as possible. And even when my husband can feel like my opponent (and vice versa), we're still sleeping in the same bed at the end of the day.

When thinking about your approach to a negotiation, consider to what extent you will be working (or living) with this person once your negotiation is done. The world is always smaller than you think; we're all connected in one way or another. Treating someone as a partner in problem-solving helps you achieve your goals, gives you a reputation as a fair negotiator, and also helps make the world a bit better.

Listening: Foundational, but Not Easy

Listening is a fundamental negotiation skill, perhaps the most important. And because it's so foundational to good negotiating, you might think it's only for undergraduate students or people new to negotiation. Hardly. Let me explain.

I practice yoga, both for my own sanity and the sanity of those around me. One of my wisest yoga teachers once said that an advanced yoga practice does not mean one has mastered the most difficult arm balances or achieved a ballerina's level of flexibility (despite what you might see on

Instagram). Rather, it means bringing an advanced level of awareness to even the most basic postures.

To achieve a basic pose like Warrior Two, for example, you need to stand with your feet apart on the yoga mat, stretch your arms straight out in either direction, bend your front knee, pivot your back foot forward about ten degrees, and hold. As if that isn't hard enough, it's just the beginning for an advanced practitioner. When you bend your knee in Warrior Two, for example, you're working to stack it directly over the ankle, so that your knee tracks over the middle toe of your foot. Your front thigh is working to get parallel to the floor, you're engaging your core, keeping your shoulders down, arms level, chest open . . . and breathing.

So, like achieving Warrior Two, listening may be foundational, but it's not at all easy. Being an advanced negotiator means bringing an advanced level of awareness to even the most foundational skills.

The most proficient negotiators are those who listen best. Research on game theory, which is the study of strategic decision-making, tells us that cluelessness, or a lack of strategic thinking, can result from a lack of sincere communication that focuses on the other person's experience. Studies show that empathic listeners not only create better connections with the people across from them, they actually maximize how much information they take and retain from a conversation. The Window section of this book will equip you to do just that. From now on, you will bring an advanced level of listening to your everyday negotiations.

How to Use the Window Section

In the Mirror section of this book, you worked to understand yourself and your situation better. You'll use the Window section of this book to do that with another person. Remember again that a negotiation is any conversation in which you are steering a relationship. So, in addition to a conversation with your boss or the other party to a contract or litigation, you'll use these second five questions in a wide range of situations, such as initiating contact with a new potential client, having a discussion with your friend or spouse, or starting a new business, before you even have a client.

You may be thinking, *Did I read that last part right?* Can I really use this section where there is no client or another person involved yet? Absolutely. If you're an entrepreneur, you know that one of your first objectives when founding a company is defining and understanding your ideal customer or target market. You need to steer that conversation with your future customer base long before you open your doors. Answering these questions on behalf of your future customer base is a fantastic way to do that. Go through the questions yourself, or with your team, and answer them as though you are the person your company is targeting. By the end of this section, you will have defined a lot about your customer that will help you move forward.

Looking Through the Window

In the Window part of the book, you're going to ask five important, open, game-changing questions of someone else, and write down the answers. But never fear: I'm not sending you in unprepared. The following five tips will help you use this part of the book to get the most out of any negotiation.

TIP ONE: LAND THE PLANE. People sometimes get nervous to ask open questions, since they feel, and are indeed, quite different from the usual types of questions we ask. Perhaps you're nervous to ask a question to which you don't yet know the answer. Or maybe you're intimidated by the thought of the silence waiting for you at the end.

But have courage. Land the plane. Meaning, you ask the question and . . . that's it.

So often people will ask a great question and then do the verbal equivalent of keeping the plane in the air while circling the airport, like, "Tell me about your kids . . . I have a couple of my own. How old are they?" You've just turned an open question ("Tell me about your kids") into a closed one that at most will get you a word or two answer ("How old are they?"). Don't wreck an open question by adding a ton of extra words, such as: "So, Sarah, what are your thoughts on our offer? You asked why the base is lower than a few of our competitors, but I think you'll see that our compensation structure allows for a lot of growth, and then there's our corporate culture . . . Have you seen our professional development programs?" If you were Sarah, would you even remember the original, open question? Doubtful. In this book, I want to teach you to steer decisively. When you ask these Window questions, don't add more; pose each question and wait. Land the plane.

TIP TWO: ENJOY THE SILENCE. Silence can be uncomfortable. So it can be scary to ask an open question, only to be met with a few seconds of silence in response. Lots of people jump back in to fill that silence with a narrow question, or worse, a judgment. It takes bravery to ask a question like the ones you're going to read in this Window section. You're asking big, open questions. Give the other person, whether they are sitting in front of you or talking to you over the phone, time to consider their answer. For the listener, silence can be a gift.

An exercise I teach in my negotiation workshops requires people to pair off, with one person speaking for three minutes, and the other listening silently. Many people cannot stay silent for three minutes. Often, they don't even know they are talking, they just do it out of habit! One executive, realizing he had failed to stay silent for a mere 180 seconds, responded by literally clapping both his hands over his mouth in embarrassment. "I know I talk over people," he said. "But I never realized how bad it was. This stops now." For the rest of the three-day workshop, I saw him sitting in silence when people spoke to him. At the end, he thanked me and said that within a matter of hours following that exercise, he already could see how much silence was going to improve his professional and personal life.

Why is it so hard for us to be silent, even for a few seconds or minutes? Often we believe we need to talk to connect with others, when silence would actually be better. Lizzie Assa, an early childhood play expert, teaches parents about the value of silence in getting kids to talk. "If parents walk in while their child is playing and say something like, 'Oh, that's pretty,' they're not connecting, they're actually making a judgment. The kids feel evaluated and clam up. Instead I like to sit in silence and observe. The more I am silently reflective, the more likely it is they will open up. Eventually the language dribbles out. Silence makes kids feel heard." Silence works for adults, too. It demonstrates respect, allows space for people to reflect on themselves and their situation, and can work more effectively than any question in encouraging people to talk.

We also talk in order to demonstrate our competence or skills, especially when we feel we're being evaluated. One executive told me, "A long time ago, when I was a new junior manager, I started holding weekly team meetings. On the occasions my director observed, I felt like I needed to show my value, so I talked a lot more. Afterward, I felt uneasy; I knew it was better when I let my direct reports lead most of the discussion. In later years, I was okay with staying silent more. Management eventually told me one of my greatest strengths was giving people space to contribute."

Finally, we talk to control a conversation and play it safe. We may have been taught that we need to know where our negotiation is going at all times, or that confidence and success in negotiation is all about having answers at the ready. But the reverse is true: it takes more confidence and skill to stay open in negotiation and hear what someone else has to say. It takes preparation, too. When you've taken the time to uncover your priorities and then listen to someone else, you'll be able to evaluate what they have said against your perspective, which leads to better solutions.

TIP THREE: FOLLOW UP. When the other person is done speaking, you may have a rush of thoughts, from reactions to specific details *you need to know right now!* Hold it. You want to keep casting a wide net. In each chapter, I'm going to give you simple, open questions you can use to follow up and get more information. These are clarification questions, which will help the other person understand more about how they think, feel, and behave, rather than just leading them to a particular answer.

TIP FOUR: SUMMARIZE AND ASK FOR FEEDBACK. You've asked an open question, listened patiently for the answer, and followed up with another open question. Now is when you *really* want to give your opinion on things. You have so much to say! Before doing so, summarize what your negotiation partner has just told you. Repeat back to them what you believe they have said, and ask for their feedback at the end.

Don't skip this step! Summarizing is one of the most powerful tools you can use in negotiation. It really drives home to the other person that you have *heard* them and digested what they had to say. Second, a summary helps both people take more from the conversation. Hearing their own words played back may allow the other person to hear information they hadn't realized before, and it enhances your memory of what the person actually said. Research shows us that when you listen in order to understand what the other person is saying, not to respond, you listen differently, and better.

We often assume we know what someone means because we understand the words they are saying to us, but frequently that is not the case. Never was this clearer to me than on my first trip to Oklahoma, eight years ago, when I arrived there for work with my colleague Shawn. After a delayed flight, we made our way to the rental car company, where a nice young man behind the counter asked me what I did for a living. When I said, "I'm a law professor," he asked me a four-word question: "What do you teach?"

I was tired. And was used to people blinking at me in disbelief when I gave this same response, since I was early in my career, a woman, and looked pretty young. So instead, I heard him ask, "What, do you teach?" Anyone who lives in New York knows what this means: "Really? *You* teach?" So in response to this totally innocent question, I barked at the guy, "Yeah. REALLY. I'm a law professor." The employee's mouth hung open in shock, and Shawn completed my embarrassment by answering from behind me, "She teaches peacebuilding!" Summarizing what someone said is a great way to test that you've actually understood what they wanted to communicate (and in doing so, avoid the embarrassment I experienced in Oklahoma).

After you summarize, you'll want to ask the other person for feedback. I like to stick with open questions, so instead of asking, "Did I get it right?" I like to summarize and then say, "What did I miss?" In this way I'm inviting the other person to let me know what else is on their mind. Often, when I ask this question, people will supplement what they originally said with something that has been on their mind but they were trying to hold back. Feedback is important, not only to make sure you have understood, but to enlarge the pie of information so that you are steering with greater accuracy.

TIP FIVE: LISTEN FOR WHAT IS _NOT_ SAID. When someone is talking, listen for everything their body is telling you. Also listen for what they don't say. You're looking for body language, the tone in which things are said, and the absence of certain words. More than 50 percent of communication is non-verbal, yet many of us have not trained ourselves to focus on anything beyond the words people speak.

One of my best students, Kate, is Korean, and introduced me to the Korean concept of _nunchi_, which literally means "eye-reading." Nunchi is the study of "reading" people's statements, actions, facial expressions, and body language, to get the fullest picture possible of what they mean and what motivates them. Michael Suk-Young Chwe, who writes about game theory, says this about nunchi:

> Even when you know a person well, it is not always easy to figure out her preferences; for example, when your mother says on the telephone that she will not be disappointed if you do not come home for the holidays, it can take substantial effort—listening to her tone of voice and interpreting her side remarks—to figure out, even imperfectly, how she

really feels. A person with good nunchi can understand another's desires when they are not expressed explicitly, can size up a social situation quickly, and can use this skill to get ahead.

In looking for body language cues, don't assume that one expression or one body position always means one thing. For example, folded arms don't always mean defensiveness; the other person may just be cold! Instead, try to observe someone's default, or baseline: their natural posture, tone of voice, or expression. Then, as you talk, watch for any changes from that baseline. If someone naturally seems to fold their arms most of the time, and then when you say something they change positions and lean forward, that tells you your words had an impact. Sometimes, I can tell that people are having a reaction to a negotiation offer because they reach for cookies sitting on the table. They may change their expression, from a frown to a smile, or vice versa. All these clues give us information that goes beyond words.

Wrapping Up

This concludes our introduction to the Window. In the following chapters, you'll learn five powerful questions that will help you gain new perspective into anyone or anything you might encounter in negotiation. And armed with the strategies in this introduction, you'll be prepared to make the most of them.

SIX

TELL ME . . .

Ben McAdams, a lifelong member of the Church of Latter-Day Saints, also known as the Mormon Church, is a first-time United States congressperson from Utah. And, unusual for a practicing Mormon, he is also a Democrat.

McAdams has spent much of his adult life working in politics in his home state of Utah. One day in 2008, he got in his car and drove to a meeting that would change his life and the lives of many in his state. And it all started with one important question.

In January of 2008, the year in which the Mormon Church helped pass California's Proposition 8, banning same-sex marriage, then Salt Lake City mayor Ralph Becker proposed a Domestic Partnership Registry whereby same-sex couples could register as partners, with the purpose of encouraging employers to approve health insurance and other partner benefits for them. Mayor Becker and McAdams hoped that this registry would help Utahns in same-sex partnerships and benefit the entire state by attracting more business to Salt Lake City. They knew there were many national companies that wanted their employees to receive benefits no matter which state they lived in.

But as they expected, the mayor's office faced serious opposition, including from within McAdams's own religion. Then senator Chris Buttars and others in the state legislature resisted the ordinance by introducing legislation that would invalidate the city's registry and prohibit municipalities from passing similar ordinances. Many people viewed the situation between the church and same-sex advocates as a war during this time period in Utah.

Some in the mayor's office despaired for the future of the registry. But McAdams believed there was a way to make it work. After Buttars introduced this legislation, McAdams, who at the time worked in the mayor's office, called Senator Buttars to set up a meeting at Buttars's home. McAdams drove to the senator's home that day with a strategy in mind. He did not demand or threaten. Instead, he decided to listen. He sat down with Buttars in his living room and simply said, "Tell me your perspective."

The two men met for three hours, most of which McAdams spent most of the time listening to Buttars's concerns. He later told *The Deseret News*, "I usually find that when I listen to others, we can find common ground." In the meeting, he learned something critically important: Buttars's primary concern was that the registry would give same-sex couples rights that opposite-sex couples didn't have. McAdams asked another question: What if we made the registry mutual, so that anyone—same-sex or opposite-sex—could register to get these benefits?

This meeting kicked off a series of negotiations that led to the creation of Salt Lake City's Mutual Commitment Registry, an ordinance with a different name but the same substance of the domestic partnership proposal. The modified ordinance was unanimously approved by the Salt Lake City Council in April 2008, with Buttars's support.

Ben McAdams's wife, Julie (herself a trained mediator), later told the press, "Buttars was worried about something that was not in the bill the way that he understood it. Ben was able to write the bill to address his particular concern, but it didn't change what Ben was trying to do. Had [Ben] not sat down and spent the time to figure out what [Buttars] was worried about, they wouldn't have gotten that far."

Casting the Widest Possible Net

Ben McAdams discovered the power of one simple, open question to transform a negotiation that profoundly affected many people in Utah. We ask questions of other people every day, and especially in negotiation. But are we asking the right ones? You already know from the Mirror section how staying curious and asking open questions can open up more information than we ever thought possible. Now we're going to learn how to do this with someone else.

For our first question, we want to start broad, and ask the question that casts the widest net. In this chapter, we'll explore the power of "Tell me." This one question invites the other person to share with you (1) their view of the goal or problem that's brought you together; (2) any important details relating to the problem or goal; (3) their feelings and concerns; and (4) anything else they feel like adding. It's the negotiation equivalent of casting a giant net into the water to see how much you can catch. This question is the most important question you should use, for any negotiation, with any person, anywhere.

"Tell Me": The Ultimate Open Question

As we explored in the introduction, "Tell me" is the most open question you can ask on any topic. It allows the person to share anything they want about themselves or a particular topic. No question unlocks trust, creativity, understanding, and mind-blowing solutions like "Tell me." Open questions like "Tell me . . ." have been called "wellsprings of innovation" because the information they produce can transform institutions as well as individuals.

Instead of sticking a line in the water and limiting yourself to one fish, you're allowing yourself the opportunity to find out a wealth of information *and* establish a positive relationship with the person across the table.

"Tell Me" Allows You to Learn the Other Person's Definition of the Problem

"Tell me" as a negotiation starter helps you get the most information possible by allowing you to hear someone else's perspective on your problem or goal. Getting this perspective requires deliberate effort, but produces so much value.

Switching perspective can be surprisingly hard to accomplish. Seeing things from another person's point of view can feel like putting on a new pair of glasses: initially it takes work and focus and may feel unpleasant before your eyes adjust. But getting that perspective is important. It helps us move from a black-and-white (and often biased) view of a situation to what some negotiation experts have called a "learning conversation," where we grow in our understanding of an issue rather than remain stuck. It gives us the best possible information from which to advocate, allows us to examine our contribution to a situation (which enables us to then change it if we desire), and empowers us to design a workable solution.

Mila Jasey is an elected member and Deputy Speaker of the New Jersey General Assembly, where for the last decade she has focused on education policy. In 2019 she won an important legislative battle on a divisive issue: salaries for school district superintendents. And she did it by taking the time to see things from someone else's perspective.

In 2011 the governor of New Jersey had instituted a salary cap for superintendents, the administrative heads of each school district, saying it would save the state money. But Mila, who had previously served on a school board, could predict the consequences: experienced superintendents immediately left New Jersey for Pennsylvania and other states, where salaries were higher, and districts found it difficult to replace them.

Increased turnover led to school budget inefficiencies, which erased most of the hoped-for cost savings. And most important, school performance suffered.

Mila saw the problems clearly, but she also knew that the salary cap had some support. So she embarked on a listening tour around New Jersey, asking families, school boards, and officials their perspective on the measure. In rural towns, she learned that even the capped amount—$175,000 per year—seemed enormous to most local families. They wondered whether more money was really necessary to attract talent. And in some of the wealthier districts, where people paid high property taxes, additional salary money felt like a burden. By sincerely listening to differing perspectives, Mila was able to generate trust and also respond effectively, acknowledging that the salaries were substantial while also focusing people on the many ways raising the cap could benefit schools, from reducing turnover to improving academic performance. She helped families think about other measures that would help contain their tax burden.

Slowly, public opinion started to change. Mila was ready to propose a bill removing the salary cap. But she needed the assembly speaker to bring it to a vote—and he wasn't sold. So Mila decided to have one more learning conversation. "Normally," Mila told me, "there's a protocol of sorts in state government, where staff only talk to staff, members only talk to members, and leadership only talks to leadership. But I had a sense of who I thought might be the most persuasive influence. So I went to the staffer I know the speaker trusts most, and we had a long, open conversation. They were concerned about appearing fiscally irresponsible. Knowing that concern helped me to make the best argument: I focused on the fact that the expected cost savings from the cap hadn't materialized." Mila waited months, but finally, one morning she got the call: the bill was coming to a vote. No one spoke out against it, not even the districts that had favored the cap. It passed by a wide margin. The years she spent engaging with other people's perceptions of the problem paid off in a major policy change.

Sometimes the Problem Isn't What You Think It Is

The beauty of "Tell me" is that sometimes it transforms your view of what a situation is about. I experienced this firsthand watching another lawyer recently when mediating an employment discrimination case, in which one party alleged he had been fired from a U.S. government agency because of racial discrimination. Months before I took the case, the parties had a contentious phone mediation that resulted in a rebuffed monetary offer and an audibly unhappy, emotional complainant. The other mediator then moved out of state, turning the case over to me. After talking with him and hearing this story, I decided to try a different tack and have the parties meet in person, on neutral ground, at our Columbia mediation office.

An agency lawyer, who had studied mediation, flew up to meet the complainant. The lawyer gave his introductory statement, but instead of asking why the complainant had turned down the agency's last monetary offer, turned to the complainant and asked, "Tell me what this case is about for you." This clearly was a different question than the complainant was expecting. What we heard next surprised us all: faced with this open question, the complainant thought about it and said, "I think what I really want is to go back to work, even if that means a smaller monetary settlement. I want to provide for my family. I want my dignity back." We ended up discussing a radically different settlement agreement, one that suited both parties better and met their interests. The two men ended mediation with a handshake, thanking each other for a productive discussion.

By starting your negotiation with "Tell me . . ." you are stepping into the other person's shoes and allowing yourself to learn from the conversation. But that's not all you get from asking this question.

"Tell Me" Builds a Relationship with the Person across from You

Terry Gross, the renowned interviewer for National Public Radio, has said that "Tell me about yourself" is the only ice-breaker you need for an interview or conversation. In a *New York Times* profile of Gross, she elaborates, "The beauty in opening with 'tell me about yourself' is that it allows you to start a conversation without the fear that you're going to inadvertently make someone uncomfortable or self-conscious. Posing a broad question lets people lead you to who they are."

When the person across from you feels as though you're making a genuine effort to understand them and their perspective, rather than just pushing your own agenda, they'll share more with you and be more open to what you have to say. "Tell me" not only allows you to see the person as they are; it also implicitly puts you on the same level as the person across from you, and invites that person into a conversational partnership with you that encourages greater trust and openness.

"Tell me" also communicates confidence in a way that helps you build rapport with your negotiation partner. The best negotiators are those who are comfortable enough to listen, stay open, and not just stick to a script of points they want to make. One of my students at Columbia received job offers from every single firm to which she applied, and while she had been a smart student, she hadn't achieved academic honors, a common prerequisite for interviewing success at the top law firms. When I asked her how she had been so successful, she told me that she had used the "tell me" prompt, asking the interviewer about themselves and their path at the organization. She said, "I wanted to hear about them at least as much as they heard about me. And after they told me about themselves and the firm, I would summarize and pick out some themes in what they said that connected up with what interested me about the firm, or what I could bring to the table. A number of those interviewers told me afterward that my interview was one of the best they'd ever had, because I had the confidence to treat the interview like we were partners in the conversation. I showed that I could listen on the spot, really understand them, and then manage a conversation successfully. And that told them I'd be successful with their clients, too."

Using "Tell Me" as the First Question in Every Negotiation

"Tell me" works as a first question not just in a formal business setting when you don't know the other person well, but also across virtually every kind of negotiation.

When Jamie, a successful family photographer with a social work background, prepares to do a photo session with a family she hasn't met before, the first question she asks is "Tell me about your family." She told me, "You'd be surprised at what you learn when you ask that question. Sometimes one parent is nervous about posing for pictures and may want some coaching, sometimes the kid has a neurodevelopmental issue that makes it hard for them to look at the camera. When I start with this question, I get the most information possible, and that helps me get to know this family and what they are hoping for from their photos."

Likewise, Amy, an experienced physical therapist, uses "Tell me" to gain a patient's trust and define treatment goals. She explains, "Lots of people are scared about physical therapy. They're worried it might hurt, or they're intimidated by the work of rehabbing from a surgery or injury. So to start out a conversation with a new client, I might ask, 'Tell me about your day-to-day,' or 'Tell me about yourself.' If they say they like to read and enjoy going to the library, but they're having trouble getting there, okay, we can work on that. The most important thing is to gain their trust. Because then we can work together. I know they'll be more likely to tell me if something hurts, or if they feel they've overdone it one week. It's important for me to know what they enjoy, what motivates them. Because if we link the work to something they love, it all becomes that much easier."

Using "Tell Me…" with Loved Ones

It takes practice to ask "Tell me . . ." of the people closest to us. Even as a trained mediator, I realized in shame one day that I had been coming home every day and asking my spouse, "How was your day?" Sometimes the response I got was, "Pretty good," and other times only a shrug as he sorted through the day's mail. Why? I was asking him a completely closed (not to mention rote) question! The day I finally decided to practice at home what I preached in the office, I arrived home from work and said, "Tell me all about your day." I was surprised at how much he opened up. He was wrapping up a difficult work project and stressed about it. The trains had been late getting into the office, but he ran into one of our classmates from law school and got a chance to catch up. He'd had a good morning workout and was feeling strong. And so on. These days, "Tell me . . ." is the number one question I ask my spouse, on almost every occasion.

I've also used this prompt with my eight-year-old daughter and remember a specific occasion when her answer to this question took me by surprise. I had taken her to a swim meet at the local pool. After a long day of swimming, she came out of the locker room in the evening in tears. I asked her what was wrong. She said, "Mom, at this pool you need to share showers. Another girl came in while I was showering. It was so awkward!" I paused for a moment. Internally, I wondered, "Could she be feeling awkward about her body? Are we at the point where she wants more privacy?" But I stayed in the moment with her, and simply asked, "Can you tell me what made it awkward?" She huffed at me. "Mom, isn't it obvious?" I said, "I'm not sure. Tell me what made it awkward for you." She responded, rolling her eyes, "We wanted our shower at different temperatures."

"Tell me . . ." allows us to hear what our partner or kids are actually thinking, instead of suggesting the answer we think is right. When sincerely asked, it also registers as genuine in a way that encourages an actual answer.

Your Turn: How to Ask This Question

Now that we know why we are asking this question—to learn more and build better relationships—we're going to work together on *how* to ask it.

You're going to ask the other person to tell you their perspective on the situation you're discussing. How exactly you pose the question depends on the type of negotiation. Here are some examples of what "Tell me . . ." can look like depending on the situation.

When You've Initiated the Negotiation

If you've initiated the negotiation, you will want to frame the issue first, and then ask the other person to tell you their perspective. Before you ask the question, you will explain the reason you asked for the conversation, as briefly as possible, and let the other person know the issue on which you'd like to hear their perspective.

For example, Brittani has asked the CEO of her start-up company to meet with her to discuss compensation. She has been with the company for a year as the VP of sales for her region, and has wildly exceeded every sales benchmark, winning several major deals that have set her company up to raise even more money. With her company heading into meetings for its next round of investors, Brittani has telegraphed to management that she'd like to discuss her results and a larger equity stake in the company. So her Window conversation may start as follows: "Thanks so much for making time for me today. I asked for a meeting because, as I think you know, I'd like to discuss my progress at the company and compensation package going forward. When I signed on last year, we had an agreement that we would review my terms after I'd been with the company for a year and we had some results to discuss. I'm very pleased with how things have gone and I'm eager to make my long-term home here. But before we get down to discussing the future, I'd love it if you could *tell me*, from your perspective, how things have gone this past year." In this way, Brittani has framed the issue in a way that sets herself up for success, but also provides an open space for her CEO to share information to round out the picture.

When Someone Else Has Initiated the Negotiation

For a meeting with a boss, client, or family member where you're not sure of the topic, you might begin by saying something like: "You asked to meet with me today. Tell me what's on your mind." Or "Tell me your hopes for this meeting."

When You've Both Agreed to Discuss a Particular Topic

If you are sitting down with someone by mutual agreement, with a specific topic in mind—for example, your performance at work or a difficult argument at home—you want to ask the broadest possible "tell me" question about that topic: "Tell me your perspective on what's been happening recently." "Tell me about the position you're looking to fill." "Tell me your thoughts on the settlement." When in doubt, a great way to start the conversation can be something as simple as "Tell me your perspective."

Land the Plane

Remember this tip from the Window introduction? Here's where you start to put it into practice. Landing the plane means that you ask your "Tell me . . ." question and then wait. Landing the plane is critically important for this question! This is your first Window question, and it's meant to be extremely broad.

Don't add another question on the end. I have seen countless people say things like, "Tell me what's brought you here . . . Have you made an offer yet?" You've taken a great open question and completely closed it. Instead of staying open to what the person had to say about their situation as a whole, you've now told them you're just here to talk numbers. Ask your question and then keep your lips closed.

Enjoy the Silence

Often we are scared of silence. We fear that we won't be prepared for what's on the other side of that silence. We fear the other person may feel pressured or burdened by the pause in conversation. But "Tell me" is a big, important question. It may take time for the other person to consider their answer. Give them that time. If you're nervous, try counting in your head while you maintain eye contact and a positive expression. Challenge yourself to see how high you can go before you break the silence. If you're on the phone, you can take this moment to stretch or just fix your gaze out the window.

You know who often requires the most time to answer this question? Kids. The first time I asked my daughter, "Tell me all about your day!" I waited for her to answer. And when I tell you I waited, I mean I waited minutes while my daughter doodled in a notebook, walked around the kitchen, and then started playing with some slime she had made at summer camp. For a moment, I thought to myself, *Well, that flopped!* But I stayed silent.

Then, slowly but surely, the trickle of information started. She'd had a substitute counselor. The sub told the kids to be quiet a lot. Someone got in trouble. She ate pizza for lunch. Could we work together on an art project? . . . And just like that, we were off to the races. Silence works.

Follow Up

If my favorite question is "Tell me," can you guess my second favorite?

"Tell me more . . ."

That's right. Let's say you've asked someone, "Tell me," and heard a bunch of information in response. After you ask someone to tell you their perspective on a situation or topic, you then will want to follow up and get more information about any valuable topics or insight they offer in response. So once you've heard the person out, you'll want to continue by summarizing what they said and then asking "Tell me more" questions about aspects of what they told you.

For example, in a conversation with a direct report about changes they'd like to make to their position at work, you might say, "So you're seeking more client contact as well as the greater feeling of autonomy you had in your previous position. Can you tell me more about that prior position?" By asking "Tell me more," you keep the person talking and get more detailed information without resorting to yes-or-no questions that shut the conversation down.

Imagine you've gone fishing off the coast of your favorite body of water. You've cast your net wide and hauled in twenty fish, along with seaweed and some other stuff. You're going to take a minute to sort through your catch and separate the fish from the stuff you're going to throw back or away. And now I want you to look at those twenty fish. Each of those fish is valuable. When you ask this question and hear some valuable information, I want you to treat each topic as a "fish" you've hauled into your net. For each topic where you'd like more information, you're going to follow up and ask the person to tell you more about that topic.

So let's say, for example, that you've asked me to tell you about my last trip to India. In response I say, "It was great! We held a Peace Summit in which we convened together ambassadors from a number of countries with Indian government leaders and some CEOs of private companies to talk about public-private partnerships for peacebuilding. My students did a fantastic job with the research and also assisted in the teaching. We stayed at a lovely hotel that had these gorgeous gardens; I tried to spend a few minutes there every day. I managed to call home every day, but sometimes my daughter was too tired to talk. That was rough, because I missed her a lot, especially in the last days of the trip. Toward the end, we spent a couple of days traveling to the Taj Mahal. Hopefully we'll be able to do this summit again every year."

Okay, you've just heard a lot of information in response to this question. Some of the things I talked about were:

- This year's Peace Summit
- My students
- The hotel and gardens

- My sadness at missing my daughter
- The Taj Mahal
- My hopes for the future of the summit

Let's say for purposes of this conversation that you're interested in talking more about the work aspects of my trip. You would then pick those topics and say, "Tell me more about the summit this year," or "Tell me more about your students' roles on the trip." If you were interested in some of the non-work parts of my trip, too, you might also ask me to tell you more about the Taj Mahal.

The purpose of "Tell me more" is to continue to keep the conversation open for as long as possible. Sometimes, people do a great job asking an initial open question, and then they narrow it precipitously in the second round. For example, you might ask me to tell you about my trip to India, and then follow up with: "How many days did the summit run?" That's a really narrow question that doesn't get you nearly as much information as "Tell me more about the summit."

If you stay with the conversation and ask "Tell me more" for the information you uncover, you'll get the most out of this question and set yourself up for success in the rest of your negotiation.

Summarize and Ask for Feedback

Next, you're going to summarize what the other person has said, and make sure you give them a chance to weigh in about it. You may think you've demonstrated to the other person that you're listening by simply sitting and hearing them out. You may also feel confident that you've heard everything they said. But if you want to make sure that you have heard all the information you need, as well as demonstrate that you have been listening, summarize what they've said after they answer. This means that you will summarize the other person's answer both after the initial "Tell me," as well as any follow-up "Tell me more" questions you ask.

Some of the greatest leaders across every profession know the value of summarizing. Recall Stephen, the law firm litigation partner from chapter 3, with the junior partner, Craig, who broke the firm's policy by filing a case in court without having run it by a litigation partner? When Stephen talked to Craig, he asked Craig's perspective on the situation, and then summarized what he had heard from Craig as follows:

"Craig, I think I understand what you've said today. The fact is, you're extremely busy, this was an important client, and it's a field of law that you know well. You've been involved in dozens of these cases, and you had studied all the laws that apply; you knew the facts cold, you had a complaint drafted that was well-researched and which you reviewed repeatedly. You weren't trying to hide anything, you just knew you had to get this done. You felt the complaint was good and that it would result in more expense for the client to run it through the required litigation partner review. You didn't want to bill your client $900 an hour for me or someone else from Litigation to look at this in light of all of the above."

When you summarize, you make sure you have learned all you can from the conversation. Stephen told me that in summarizing Craig's perspective, he understood in a new way what Craig was thinking about the situation. In addition, Stephen's summary reduced Craig's defensiveness and put Craig in a frame of mind to really hear what Stephen had to say.

After you summarize, you'll ask the other person for feedback. Again, I like to do this by asking, "That's everything I have in my notes. What did I miss?" By asking for feedback, I make sure that I learn the most possible from the conversation, and that the other person knows that I really want to hear them.

Stephen asked Craig for feedback on the summary above. And when he did, Craig added some information—while he didn't consult with a litigation partner, he had asked a very competent litigation associate to work with him on the case—that helped Stephen understand the situation more fully. Stephen summarized this additional information, and thanked him for adding it. After having his feedback heard, the junior partner visibly relaxed and Stephen was able to share the firm's concerns with much greater success.

Asking for feedback is the last critical step in making sure we have heard and understood the other person's perspective on the situation at hand. It sets us up for success when we eventually turn to thinking about the future, and what steps we want to take.

Listen to What's Not Said

When you ask this question, you'll want to pay attention to the other person's expression and body language as they are answering the question and giving you feedback. Stephen told me that Craig looked extremely tense when they first sat down. He could see by the furrow in Craig's brow and his crossed arms that Craig might be feeling defensive. When Stephen started to summarize, Craig relaxed a little bit but also leaned forward and pressed his hands together. That told Stephen that Craig might have more to say. When Stephen gave Craig the chance for feedback and summarized the additional information, Craig smiled for the first time and leaned back in his chair. Stephen could see by Craig's expression and body language that, finally, Craig had felt completely heard.

Wrapping Up

You've learned to ask a terrific open question, followed up, summarized, and asked for feedback. Your negotiation is off to a great start. Now let's continue the conversation in a way that will start to produce ideas for your eventual solution.

SEVEN

WHAT DO YOU NEED?

A senior television executive flew across the country, ready to start what she expected to be a heated legal negotiation over one of the television programs in her portfolio.

The program in question centered around a comedy act. Just after going live with the program, her network got hit with an unwelcome surprise: a small content producer, a husband-and-wife team with a comedy act that had been playing on local TV elsewhere in the country, sued for trademark infringement. Their small program had been on the air for two years, and the couple felt the network was trying to profit off public awareness and their reputation by using a similar name.

The network immediately changed the title of their comedy program. But the couple refused to drop the suit. The resulting litigation had dragged on, heavily costing both parties, and had led to the television executive's flying across the country for a mediation, designing a strategy for how to approach the meeting with the other side. She knew the company's position: *Not one dime. We can take this to trial and win.*

She arrived at the mediation with her army of lawyers, sat down, and

saw the husband-and-wife team on the other side, sitting with their lawyer. Reviewing the plan she'd hatched on the plane, she looked across the
table and asked the couple if they would be willing to talk to her without
any lawyers in the room. The couple looked at each other, paused, and
agreed. After all the lawyers (nervously) filed out, she turned to the couple
and asked them a single question:

"What do you need?"

This question seemed to both stun and relieve the couple. They
thought for a moment and then told the executive, "We just love the
program we've created. This is our passion project. We sued because we
feared we wouldn't survive. What we need now more than anything else is
exposure. Otherwise, that fear may come to pass." The executive thought
about it and made an offer: How about a few advertising spots on one of
the other TV channels she was responsible for overseeing? She had a few
upcoming spots that no advertisers had bought yet; it would cost her network very little but would represent significant value to the local comedy
group by providing broad exposure they otherwise could not afford on
their own. The couple looked astonished when she revealed this offer, and
quickly accepted. The two sides settled the case. As the executive headed
to the airport, she received a text from the wife with a note of thanks and
some book recommendations for her flight.

This one question opened up a whole negotiation. As the network
had hoped, the executive settled the case for a zero-dollar payout. But
her question generated so much more than just a mediation agreement.
Shocked and impressed by this executive's creative, collaborative approach, the couple stayed in touch and eventually became good friends
with her. Later on in her career, when the executive was seeking to make a
career move, the couple connected her with some people in their network.

This one question transformed the situation, and the executive's life,
in a way she never expected.

Asking about Needs: A Game-Changer in Negotiation

This story, where "What do you need?" transformed a tense moment between a network executive and husband-and-wife team, is what originally inspired me to write this book. It demonstrates the ability of a single question to turn a contentious situation into an opportunity for lifelong mutual gain.

Asking "What do you need?" is a life changer. It helps you access the reasons why people do what they do. It's much easier to negotiate from someone's underlying need than their demand. Think about the above case: the couple's position was, "You stole our title for your own gain. You owe us damages." The large company's position was, "We didn't steal your title. And moreover, you can't show that you suffered any damages. We owe you nothing." Had they just stuck to their positions, they would have ended up with a very different, costlier, and less productive result.

Getting underneath someone's demands to figure out the needs driving them can help transform someone's ideas about a conflict and what to do with it. The fact is that needs, not rights, are the real reason many people initiate lawsuits. Needs, not rights, are the reason many negotiations stall out or end badly. They are the person's *why*, the reason for taking the position they do. And when we figure out someone else's needs, those needs help us generate much better solutions to tough problems.

Practice Identifying Needs

How often have you sat across from someone, even someone you know very well, and asked them what they need? Most of us, seasoned negotiators included, need some practice in asking this question and then listening—really listening—to the answer. Especially because, over time, we see a lot of the same demands popping up again and again, so it's easy to assume they'll have similar solutions. But once you dig deeper, you'll most likely find that the parties' individual needs are very different.

My Columbia students and I mediate a lot of employment disputes involving the U.S. government, and the difference in outcome between two similar cases—for example, where a woman has been denied a promotion and sues for sex discrimination—shows just how varied a negotiated agreement can be for the same initial problem.

Let's imagine two women from Agency X arrive simultaneously at my office. Each of them has the same position: "Alex, I was denied a promotion purely because I am a woman." I invite in the first woman, who repeats her position. We ask her, "What do you need?" and she says, "Because I was denied that promotion, I couldn't provide for my son's medical and special needs educational therapies."

Her needs here are monetary. Of course she has other needs as well—any parent out there knows that the only way you can sleep at night is to know you did your best to provide for your child—but her primary, tangible need in this case is money. This negotiation likely ends with a monetary settlement.

Now the second woman comes in. Again, she states her position: "I was denied a rightful promotion because I'm a woman." We ask her, "What do you need?" and she tells us, "I need what happened to me to never happen to another woman ever again." Her need varies greatly from the first woman's; she needs institutional change. For this plaintiff, we might end up with a managerial training program aimed at gender equity in the workplace. A similar position does not have to equate to identical needs.

Uncovering underlying needs also works wonders for relationship issues. Perhaps your partner has spent years telling you something like, "You never remember to clean out the sink and load the dishwasher before we go to bed!" Chances are this leads to a response like, "I just did it yesterday—and besides, I'm exhausted! I put out the trash and helped with homework. What else do you want from me?"

Again, this is a fight centered entirely on demands. When you ask a question that focuses instead on your partner's needs, you might hear something different. I once worked through this with a couple, and it turned out that what the person who valued a clean sink actually *needed* was a feeling of peace and harmony when she came downstairs in the morning. The sink just did that for her. If she saw a clean sink and counter, she could relax and breathe as she started her day. The partner started to see that his spouse's need was actually not about controlling him—it was about controlling her anxiety. In turn, her partner needed some flexibility for unusually busy nights. After discussing their needs, the couple decided that if they needed to make a choice, they would forgo the trash collection and focus instead on tidying the kitchen. They also gained a greater understanding of each other that helped keep things happier around the home.

Identifying the underlying needs helps us avoid cookie-cutter negotiations and create innovative, durable, and specific solutions that work for the people involved. Never make the mistake of assuming that you know what someone's needs are just because their demand sounds familiar.

Your Turn: Asking about Someone's Needs

You've already started this conversation as openly as possible by asking the other person "Tell me . . ." and listening to the answer. Now you're ready to ask the question "What do you need?"

Feel free to personalize this question in a way that makes sense for your negotiation. For example, if you're approaching a buyer at Target to sell your home product, you could ask, "What do you need from your vendors?" or "What do you need from this deal?" If you're negotiating with your spouse over the home budget and whether one of you can book that expensive vacation: "When we're thinking about how we prioritize our money, what do you need?" If you're sitting down with that bathroom contractor: "What do you need when you work with homeowners?" or "What do you need to get this job done?"

Land the Plane

Even seasoned professionals, or longtime couples, hesitate to ask an open question about needs. It feels deeper, riskier, *different* from the usual types of questions we ask. I see so many negotiators ask this question and then metaphorically circle the airport with a string of words like, "What do you need? I feel like earlier in our relationship you wanted . . ." "What do you need here? How about we move this number . . ." Don't worry about asking this question as is, don't add your own judgments, and also don't think you know better than the person sitting across from you. Be brave. Ask your four-word question and land the plane.

Enjoy the Silence

Then, leave room for silence for the other person to consider and answer your question.

Follow Up

Sometimes when you ask someone what they need, you may get a short or vague answer, such that you'd like to follow up—but don't do it with a narrow question or, worse, your idea for a solution! You'll be closing off the flow of information just when you stand to gain the most. Instead, remember my trip to India, and say, "Thanks. Can you tell me more about _____?"

The follow-up question is where so many people go wrong, remembering to ask the big question but then losing their discipline for the follow-up. Instead, try our handy "Tell me more." This is particularly helpful if you ask, "What do you need?" and someone says, "I don't know." In the process of asking for more information in a broad way, you can help someone clarify with, "Okay, so you're not sure what you need. Maybe tell me more about what's running through your mind right now." Then enjoy the silence once more.

Two main buckets of needs come up when you ask this question that may look familiar from earlier in the book: intangibles and tangibles. Let's talk about how to follow up on each.

Dealing with Intangibles

You've asked a question about needs. We know from research and practice that asking about needs yields deep-seated, important information that can unlock a deal or a conflict. Many needs, however, are intangibles (as you found out for yourself in chapter 2), meaning they are conceptual instead of concrete. Which leads us to our important follow-up question that, as you did for yourself in chapter 2, you're going to ask next: *What would that look like?*

"What would that look like?" helps the person you're talking to bring their needs to life and visualize what they could look like in reality. It helps them look to the future and picture what they most want to see. Finally, this question opens a window between you and the person you're talking to, and gives you important details that can be critical in finding a mutual path forward. When you ask this critical question, you help the person sitting across from you bring their needs into the realm of the concrete and give you powerful clues about potential solutions to the issue between you.

A health coach sat down with her client, whom she'd been working with for about a year. The client, a professional woman, was a dedicated yoga practitioner who suffered from emotional eating and had grown frustrated that every year since she turned forty, despite all her efforts, the scale had crept up a pound or two until her clothes no longer fit. In the initial meeting with her coach, the woman had identified a weight-loss goal of twenty pounds. She had access to high-quality fresh foods, a gym membership—everything she needed to reach her goal. She started working to eat healthier. She dropped her yoga classes and vigorously exercised five to six times a week, including weight training. And yet, the scale seemed to be stuck within a pound or two of her original weight. The more the number refused to move, the more this client fixated on it. Finally, the client expressed her frustration and despair to her coach—who responded immediately and scheduled a meeting.

This time, the coach took a different approach. She asked her client to put aside the weight for a minute and think about what she *needed*. The client responded immediately, "I need to feel healthier and more in balance." The coach replied, "Great. You need to feel healthy and in balance. What would that look like?" The client thought for a moment, and then responded, "I don't know . . . I think I need more rest, and I think I miss yoga. That was my sanity, and now I'm doing other stuff in an attempt to lose weight, but it just leaves me feeling more tired. Between work, grocery shopping, exercise, and my kids, I'm so exhausted that I find myself eating at night just to stay awake."

Now the coach and the client had information they needed to move forward. By asking this question, the coach helped her client access her inner wisdom and self-diagnose the solution to the problem. Together, they focused on rest and balance. By setting an earlier bedtime and coming up with a relaxing evening routine, they helped the client cut down on her late-night eating. They integrated some yoga classes back into her exercise routine and helped her achieve balance between that and cardio workouts. They also brainstormed some meal-prep shortcuts to help the client feel less burdened. With the pressure off and some balance restored, the client started to feel better and lose weight at a slow, sustainable pace. All of this came from asking one question that helped both the coach and the client herself conceptualize what health and balance looked like to achieve her goal.

I love the "What would that look like?" question and ask it in virtually every negotiation scenario—but most negotiators don't even know this question exists. Or if they do, they can't ask it. Why? Because they haven't first found out from the other person what they need, as you just did. Here is where you start to see your earlier work in posing broad questions and listening—really listening—to the answers, pay off.

When you get to this question, you are going to ask it by first reflecting back what you heard as the person's needs, and then asking them what that would look like. As an example, if you're talking to one of the owners of a thriving bakery: "You know, Ilan, I heard you say earlier that one of your biggest needs was feeling recognized at work for your expertise. What would that look like here?" Then, you're going to continue to reflect back his words and ask for more information using a "What else?" question. So when Ilan responds, perhaps by saying, "I'd like the bakers in our store to take my direction on our product, rather than just nodding and then asking my husband," you can respond with, "Okay, so you'd like to know that when you give advice to your bakers, they will follow it first, without needing to check with your husband. What else would recognition at work look like?"

The openness of this question is so important because it allows you to dig into what the other person sees for their (and perhaps your shared) future. Here is where, once more, we must resist the urge to tack on narrow follow-on questions at the end. Those questions often reflect our *assumptions* about the person or the situation—which may be very far from the reality. If your tween girl says she needs more freedom at home, hold yourself back from saying, "What would more freedom look like? Wait, is this about getting an iPhone again?" As the parent of a tween girl myself, I can rarely predict what's on my daughter's mind. Disciplining myself to listen to her has made us so much closer as I get to know the person she is, and is becoming.

This question is also important if you are facing a negotiation with what I call a counterpuncher. You know, the person who has shot down every single one of your ideas, saying, "That's not going to work," without so much as one positive suggestion of their own? That one. When you ask them a question that puts the ball in their court—like, "What would a workable solution look like?"—and then patiently enjoy the silence that follows, you are forcing—ahem, inviting—them to actively participate in the search for a solution.

Dealing with Tangibles

And if you get tangibles when you ask this question (as an example, "I need you to report your results to me by telephone twice a week"), then you know how you're following up: "Help me understand: What makes the twice-weekly call important?"

Once someone has stated a tangible need, we use this follow-up question to get a deeper understanding of the intangible need behind it.

Again, avoid asking "Why is that important?" Instead of *why* ask, "What made/makes . . . ?" or just "Tell me . . ." Especially if there is any difficulty or previous patterns of unsatisfactory communication, *why* can seem confrontational or aggressive. Social workers rarely ask *why* questions because they are looking to increase trust and rapport. For example, compare "Why don't you want to cancel your golf membership when you know we are struggling financially?" with "What makes the golf membership important for you?" You can see which question is more likely to produce a constructive answer.

In this way, the colleague who asked you to report your results to them by telephone twice a week will be able to clarify what that report represents. Will it help them communicate better with the board of directors? Or is it that they need to feel more in the loop and have the security of knowing what's going on? We're trying to get at the need that's underneath the tangible they just listed, so that you understand the problem they're trying to solve and can start to troubleshoot potential solutions. If they say they need the reports to be in the loop, but you know that twice a week won't work for a particular reason, you now have some ideas for a path forward. Eventually, once you have finished summarizing and given them an opportunity for feedback, you might acknowledge their need to be in the loop, describe the challenges with the suggested phone reports, and then ask them what ideas they have, or propose some ideas yourself, for other ways you could work together to meet this need.

Another example is a vice president at a Fortune 100 company in New York who was offered, one year into her job, responsibility for an additional business unit. The promotion didn't include a title change, but the role would have a significantly higher profile than before, and require a lot of travel to the West Coast. She went back and forth with her company on salary, and relatively quickly reached the maximum they could give for this position (which she verified with some research). She told them that she needed more value from the deal, to which they responded,

"We hear that. We've hit the maximum on the compensation. How else can we help you get some value here?" The executive thought about it. This new job, which she wanted, would mean significantly more travel away from her husband. She would be away twice a month, for a week each time. She went back and asked them for her husband to be able to join her once a month, with his airfare, hotel, and daily expenses paid. That "value" came out of a different pot of money from the compensation pot. They quickly agreed, and she had a deal.

If you know that you're going to have trouble meeting someone's tangible need, one great strategy forward is to uncover the intangible that's beneath it, and then (after you've completed the questions!) ask how else you could help them with their need.

Summarize and Ask for Feedback

After asking your question, honoring the silence, and following up with more open questions, it's time to repeat back what you heard. Summarizing ensures that you have heard the person who is talking with you and that you've digested what they had to say. In particular, having one's needs heard can be incredibly cathartic.

One of the exercises my mentor, Carol Liebman, taught me is a listening exercise where we have trainees break out into groups and listen to one another describing a conflict they are experiencing. After they finish, their fellow group members will, among other things, summarize what they need. I ran this exercise in a recent training I conducted for civil rights lawyers, and afterward, the department head pulled me aside to say, "Alex, I know you came here to train us in mediation, but I just experienced something even more powerful. I'm dealing with a thorny work conflict that's been keeping me up at night. Having someone actually *hear* my needs and summarize them for me induced in me the most profound feeling of relief I can ever recall experiencing. It was as though it put gas back in my tank to get to work and actually solve the problem. I'm going to go back to my office and do that right now!" So the first benefit for the other person of having their needs heard and summarized is it makes them feel respected and heard.

Summarizing what someone needs also may give them information that they may not have understood before. I summarized once for Andrea, a businessperson who was having a conflict with her younger brother, Chad. After Chad went through a rough financial period, Andrea had bought him an apartment and brought him into her business as an employee. She told me she now regretted it; Chad had gotten into a relationship with someone who had a criminal record for assault as well as illegal financial dealings; all of a sudden, he was buying cars he couldn't possibly afford and talking about bringing his girlfriend into the company, too. Andrea talked to me about the importance of maintaining a spotless reputation for the health of her business, and finished by saying, "I think I may need to step away and just not see him socially for now."

I said, "You've told me you regret bringing Chad into the business, and your reputation is very important to you. I wonder if you need to take a break from him in the business arena, too."

She nodded. "I didn't want to think about that, but I do."

Summarizing also has powerful effects for you, the listener. By forcing you to listen in a different way, it increases your understanding of what the person actually said. So often we listen with half our attention or through the lens of our own experience, but listening to understand what the other person is saying, rather than to respond, helps you listen differently and better.

You also have a chance to test your understanding of what the person actually said when you summarize. If you thought you heard that your client needed more frequent email communication, and what they actually needed was communication only when certain substantive or personnel changes were being considered, that's an important distinction. This last step gives you a chance to make sure that you've heard what the other person intended you to hear.

Always end a summary by asking for the other person's feedback. Feedback lets you know how you did. Avoid "Did I get that right?" because it's fishing with a line, inviting a simple yes or no answer. Instead, ask for feedback in a way that lets the listener know you expect and welcome it, such as "How'd I do?" or even "What did I miss?" Then give the person your full attention and patience once again.

Listen for What Is *Not* Said

Sometimes when you ask someone this question, they will flat-out tell you their needs. But sometimes, uncovering what someone needs requires listening carefully between the words for what they mean, including non-verbal cues. If, for example, I summarize and then ask someone, "Did I get that right?" and they have a questioning or reluctant tone, a frown, a head shake, or a downward look, those may be signs that I've left something unexplored. In that case, I usually say something like, "It looks like I did miss something after all—please tell me how I can understand better."

You've now asked someone else about their needs. You've helped them make those needs concrete or connected those tangible needs to something greater. You've summarized what the person has said and asked for feedback. You've also looked for non-verbal communication and invited the person to be as open as they wish.

Now let's move on to the next question, where I'm going to give you a simple, effective, "no therapist couch necessary" way to ask someone about their emotions—like you did for yourself in chapter 3.

EIGHT

WHAT ARE YOUR CONCERNS?

Rahul walked into his boss's office to start what he feared would be a tough conversation. Six months earlier, seeking a new challenge beyond his domestic portfolio of work, he had applied for and been named vice president of his company's international division, in charge of operations. He was a dynamic young leader with a management style that inspired his millennial staff. The president of the international division had spent his career in that division and was promoted when the previous president became CEO of the entire company.

Once Rahul arrived in his new position, the challenges of running the international division became apparent. International markets were experiencing the brunt of fluctuations happening across the world, and Rahul's specific company, a veteran in an industry with increasingly strong competition from new players, was struggling. One week earlier Rahul, a new divisional vice president, and his boss had a tense meeting with the company's CFO, Arya, who had looked over their personnel chart and asked why a certain category of positions needed to exist, since they didn't on the domestic side. There was a moment of silence before Rahul said, "That's an interesting question. I'll take a look at it."

Recalling this interaction later, he told me, "In that moment, after my exchange with Arya, I saw my boss look at me with an expression I couldn't really read. Initially, I thought things were fine, but over the next week his communications to me were much shorter and less frequent than usual. Things just seemed off . . . like he was hurt by my response." He continued, "So I went to see him in his office. I really wanted to ask my boss what he was feeling, but I was afraid to be so blunt about it. I thought it might put him on the defensive, like I was calling him emotional. Instead I said, 'It might just be me, but I feel like things have been off between us since that conversation with Arya last week. I want to understand your concerns.'"

Rahul's boss opened up. He told Rahul that his job performance was terrific, but that he needed to feel like Rahul was on his team. The president felt extremely loyal to his staff, many of whom had also grown up in the international division, like him (and unlike Rahul). He had hoped Rahul would help him articulate the unique needs of their division to Arya, or even reserve comment until they could come up with a strategy together, rather than immediately entertaining the idea of cutting international staff just because they didn't exist on the domestic side. As the president was talking, Rahul listened to his soft tone and figured something else out: the previous international president had been a larger-than-life presence in the office, who was outgoing and commanded a room. This new president, Rahul's boss, was a quiet man, brilliant with data but more reserved in personal interactions. Listening to him, Rahul realized that he had been hired in part to fill in the areas where the president felt less strong—but that only worked as long as he felt they were operating under one purpose. Otherwise, Rahul realized, he might come across as wanting the president job himself, which was not the case. He was learning a great deal in this role, and his preference was to stay on the operations side rather than assume total responsibility for this division.

Rahul summarized his boss's concerns and thanked him for his candor. He thanked his boss for taking a chance on him in this role and shared how much he had been learning. Together, they worked to educate Arya about the roles of international staff, while privately making contingency plans in case the company insisted on cuts. They also made a plan for future interactions with Arya. Things felt better around the office. They were once again on the same team.

Asking about Someone's Concerns

The next step in your negotiation is to ask the person about their concerns. Hearing people's concerns will help you in any negotiation. Not only does it help you get information that will be critical to your negotiation but it also has the powerful effect of making the other person feel heard.

Asking about someone's concerns is the best way to understand and address any lingering concerns about you or your business that might prevent a successful deal. People often won't share their concerns with you upfront. Instead, they'll leave them unsaid, and leave your negotiation unresolved, or give someone else their business. But when you ask someone about their concerns, you give yourself the best possible chance of reaching success in your negotiation.

Second, asking about someone's concerns is a great way of getting at their needs. This is especially useful when you are meeting someone for the first time, or are trying to win over a new client. This question will help you uncover what needs aren't being met and explain how you can meet them.

Last, getting at someone's concerns is a great way of discovering their feelings about a situation without using what I call the "F-word" and putting a person on the spot.

Addressing Barriers to Agreement

Addressing someone's potential concerns with you or what you're propos-
ing helps you eliminate any barriers to agreement. It gives you good data
on why a resolution has not already been reached with this person—what
has been holding someone back. Many times, our clients, spouses, and colleagues will not make their concerns clear. They may be waiting for permission, an opening to say it's okay. If you don't ask, they won't tell, and you
may not reach an agreement. So you need to invite them—in the right way.

I once talked to a company about a potential speaking engagement.
This company had never brought in an outside speaker to coach them in
negotiation, instead relying exclusively on their in-house trainers. When
we spoke about my coming in, I asked them directly, "I know you have an
in-house training team. What concerns do you have about bringing in an
outside speaker?" They literally exhaled in relief. "I'm so glad you asked,"
said the senior manager on the call. "Historically, we've had a couple of
concerns. One was about price and whether we could justify the additional expense to senior management. But the other was about what it
might signal to our employees. Because we normally use our in-house
training team, we didn't want them to feel devalued, or our employees to
get the message that something was seriously wrong and that's why we
hired a big speaker from the outside."

This information helped me structure a proposal for this company that
met their needs. I made sure to include all the companies I had trained
that also had in-house training teams, so that management could tell their
employees that most companies now found it valuable to get some outside
expertise on negotiation. I also included bullet points on why many companies were choosing to hire outside speakers on negotiation to train even
their internal trainers—that this kind of training could help anyone, including trainers, advance their careers within their companies. And I gave
management ideas for how I could involve their in-house trainers in my
session, so that we were also celebrating the expertise in the room. Asking
their concerns gave me valuable information that helped me land the deal.

In addition to helping you address any barriers to agreement, the other reason to ask what concerns someone has with you or what you are offering is that it builds rapport and it encourages openness. It shows that you simultaneously possess enough confidence to address any concerns that may come up, and that you care about making sure what you are offering is right for this deal. One successful art buyer told me that she has built credibility over the years by making sure she hears her clients' concerns. If a piece of art she has identified for that client doesn't meet those concerns, she advises them not to buy, despite the fact that she would earn a commission. She tells people to wait for something that will meet their needs in the long term. And in doing so, she has earned the lifelong loyalty—and commission dollars—of her clients.

Addressing Unmet Needs

Asking someone about their concerns helps you understand any needs they have that aren't being met, or what's not working for the person as things stand. If you're looking to secure a new client or deal, you will want to know what didn't work in the last deal they did. So you can ask, "What were your concerns about your last deal?" In this way, you'll understand better what their priorities and needs are, and you'll be positioned to do better for them.

Elizabeth is an insurance broker who advises families with large businesses or property holdings on their insurance needs. One day, she and her team walked into a conference room for a meeting with a prospective client, a family with substantial insurance needs, in hopes of winning their business. The family had been with another insurance broker for a while and said things were "fine," but yet they had asked for this meeting.

Elizabeth's team started the meeting by introducing their company and talking about what they could offer. Elizabeth, who had been watching the family and sizing up the situation, paused the presentation to ask the family a question: "Before we go any further, I want to make sure we are responsive to your needs. What are your concerns about your current situation?"

The family said they were concerned about the level of service they were receiving from their current broker. Elizabeth summarized and followed up: "So the level of service hasn't been what you needed. Can you tell us more?" They elaborated. Their current broker was working part-time. Sometimes they would try to reach her and she wasn't in—and they had to wait a few days for help. They didn't feel as though they had someone who was taking care of them and prioritizing their concerns.

Insurance brokers normally put together proposals for potential clients that look like spreadsheets, with a number of different policies listed and the numbers for each. But at the conclusion of the meeting, Elizabeth put together a service plan that showed the family who would have primary responsibility for their account, including backup personnel in case that person was out. After she sent it over, the family spokesperson called her and said, "Wow, this is different from what we usually see. I've never seen a proposal that focused on service." The family awarded Elizabeth's company their full account. Not only did Elizabeth's question help her win the business, it won the family's trust. When Elizabeth changed companies a few years later, the family called and said, "We're going with you."

Getting to the Root of Someone's Feelings

"What are your concerns?" is a really effective way of asking about someone's feelings without using the "F-word" itself. We know how critical feelings are to unlocking conflict and reaching deals. But a lot of us have strong reactions to the "F-word," whether in work or relationships. It can be difficult to ask a coworker, someone you don't know well, or someone with whom you may be having a conflict, what they are feeling without provoking defensiveness. Many people in negotiations are not ready to confront their own emotions when asked about them by another person. And to make things worse, people often ask a more closed version of the feelings question—"Are you upset with me?"—that at best gets limited information and instead, frequently inflames the conversation. When you ask someone about their concerns, you give them an open, safe prompt to talk about their feelings.

Consider Rahul's story from the beginning of this chapter. He sensed that something was wrong in his relationship with his boss. He could have just made a plan with his boss to address Arya's concern, but it wouldn't have fixed the real issue, which was the CEO's wanting to feel like a team. Rahul's asking about his CEO's concerns paved the way for them to address the root issue, rather than cycling through potential solutions to an unknown problem. Because they addressed this underlying concern, they fixed their working relationship in addition to formulating a plan to talk to the CFO.

Trainer Autumn Calabrese told me a story about how addressing a client's concerns helped her negotiate with him and make progress toward his goals. Autumn works with a small number of high-profile clients on personal training and nutrition for weight loss. One day, she used this question to negotiate with one of her clients, a successful and overweight man in his thirties who was working on his fitness and nutrition in order to get healthier. Autumn said, "One day we were working out and something major came up. Because he was significantly overweight, over four hundred pounds, exercise was hard for him. Up until that point, we had just been working out. But that day, I had him do one particular exercise move, and then I could see it. There was anger coming out of him. The more we would do the workout move, the more he would get mad and frustrated with himself—and the more you get mad and frustrated, the more that your form can slip, meaning you're not doing the move right. That can lead to injury, so I had to stop him. I said, 'What's going on? What is concerning you?' He said, 'I'm mad because I can't do it.' I said, 'I don't think that's what you're mad about.' And we sat there. For a minute he said, 'Forget it, I'm not going to do this,' but I said to him, 'You're not walking out of the gym. Sit down. Tell me what's concerning you.' And what came out surprised us both. He had lost his parents when he was very young, and his grandfather had raised him. When he was ten years old, he went in the bedroom in the morning to get ready for school and found his grandfather had passed away. Because of that, over a yearlong period he went into foster care, where he went through a lot of traumatic stuff. There were several kids in the house, and his foster parents would lock the refrigerator at night so they could only eat at certain times."

As Autumn told me, he developed a bad relationship with food as a result of this traumatic event. So years later, at thirtysomething years old, what was happening during this workout was that all his sadness about losing his grandpa, the emotions that came along with going into foster care, and the way he was abused around food and eating that he had suppressed for all those years, bubbled to the surface. She added, "And so he got it out, and then we got back to the workout, because we had addressed some of the real work. Asking about his concerns let us both figure out that it wasn't about a lunge or because the weights were heavy—there was something much bigger there under the surface. Addressing it helped him, and us, get back on the right foot toward his goals." Autumn used this one open question to help her negotiate her relationship with her client so he could continue to work toward a healthier future.

How to Ask the Question

In the rest of this chapter, we will discuss how to ask someone about their concerns effectively. I will give you tips to set the stage and then deal with some of the reactions you might get to this question. I will also help you work through what to do when you have accurately summarized how someone is feeling, but they're not ready to hear it from you. And I will give you strategies for how to handle feedback from the other person once you have summarized their answer.

Land the Plane

This question is one where you may be nervous to bring the plane down for a landing. Asking someone about their concerns invites them to tell you something you may not agree with or like—or something for which you may not feel totally prepared. But take heart. First of all, the person may not have concerns about you but about something or someone else. Wouldn't that be great to know? Second, if the person has concerns, it's much better to know than not. It allows you a chance to address them and close your deal, instead of letting them fester and get in the way of your negotiation. Don't try to guess someone's concerns or close off the conversation. Ask the question and land your plane. And remember, following the tips below means that you don't even need to come up with an answer to those concerns immediately. You have time to gather information and formulate a plan.

Enjoy the Silence

After you ask this question, you're going to enjoy (or at least allow) the silence that may follow. This question in particular might take someone an extra beat or two to answer. Do not jump in to fill what may feel like dead air—because that air isn't dead, it's alive with great possibility. What comes out on the other end of that silence may change everything you know about the negotiation and the other person.

Follow Up

When you ask someone about their concerns, you may uncover some of their feelings or unmet needs that they didn't share before. For example, when Elizabeth asked this question of her prospective clients, they told her they needed better service. One of the best ways to follow up and hear more about those needs is to summarize (see next page) and then ask, as she did, "Can you tell me more about that?" In this way, you'll help them (and yourself) make those needs concrete so that you can address them in your negotiation. In this case, Elizabeth found out that better service meant knowing that someone would always be in to return their call if they had a business need.

Summarize and Ask for Feedback

Again, you'll want to summarize what you hear when you ask this question. By repeating back what you've heard and giving the other person an opportunity to weigh in, you'll also help them (and you) hear what they have said and make any corrections or additions they wish. Finally, summarizing also helps the other person know their concerns were important enough that you took the time to understand them.

Listen to What Is *Not* Said

I've asked you to pay attention to non-verbal language throughout these Window questions, but when you're asking someone their concerns, you must pay attention to what isn't said. Sometimes that means reading between the lines of what someone is telling you about their concerns, to figure out what's really bothering them. Paying attention to non-verbal communication is *crucial* when you ask about someone's concerns. People frequently censor their concerns in negotiation unless directly invited—sometimes multiple times—to share them. I can't tell you the number of times I have asked someone if a particular proposal will work for them and they say yes *while shaking their head no*! Nikhil Seth of the United Nations told me that asking about someone's concerns is extremely important in diplomatic negotiations and that the answer to the question may not be stated verbally. "You have to interpret the person's emotive language—it may not be verbal, but instead may be from what I call the 'eyes of the body'—to see how people really feel about a certain issue."

So when you ask someone about their concerns, you want to be extremely attentive to body language as well as tiny wording clues that tell you they may be holding back on their concerns or experiencing something they are reluctant to share. When this happens, I respond by (1) respectfully noting the verbal and non-verbal communication I'm seeing; (2) stating my respect for this person and her viewpoint; and (3) re-asking the question. As a mediator, I've asked people many times what concerns they have about a particular deal. If they shrug, look down and say, "Yeah, this is fine," that tells me that "fine" means "less than good," and the shrug may indicate resignation. I might respond, "Your words are telling me we're fine, but your face is saying something different. You're the decision-maker here, not me, so if you have concerns, I want to understand them. What did I miss?" They appreciate this and add whatever I didn't get the first time.

Even your loved ones, whether family or other close relationships, may hold back on sharing their concerns out of fear or embarrassment. My brother and sister-in-law recently welcomed a baby girl. At our first big family gathering after her birth, I could tell that my daughter, who for many years had been the only child in our extended family, was struggling with the shift in everyone's attention. During a quiet moment, I asked her what she was feeling, and she said, "Nothing, Mom! I'm fine. I'm just tired from the trip." I tried again. "I know you're telling me you're fine, but your face looks a little sad. If anything is bothering you, even if it's just a tiny bit, you can tell me." This time, she snuggled in for a hug and told me that she loved her baby cousin but felt like maybe she didn't matter as much to the adults in our family anymore. We had a meaningful conversation in which I was able to share that as the oldest child in my family, I too had struggled with feeling left behind when my siblings were born. Listening to what she didn't say and inviting her to be open with me helped pave the way for us to connect.

What about if you ask this question and meet some resistance? Let's say I ask someone, "What's concerning you?" and they push their chair back, cross their arms, and say, "I'm not sure what you're talking about." This is a sign they may be feeling defensive or worried you may try to put them on the spot. (Note that they may also be feeling one or both of the "Big Two": fear and guilt.) If this happens to you, here's something to try: remember in the Mirror question about feelings, how I told you a story about myself before I asked you to return the favor? You're going to do that here, the way Rahul did in the story that began this chapter, when he led with his own concerns before asking his boss to reciprocate. So as an example, I might respond with, "I feel like that question didn't land the way I intended. Let me try again: for the last week, I've been concerned about the way things have felt between us. I found myself concerned that something had gone wrong, and I didn't know what. I greatly value what you have to say. So I'm here to listen to anything that may be concerning you." Chances are that by respecting their initial hesitation and showing a little of your own humanity, you'll be more successful in this second attempt.

If you do this, and the person still insists they don't have concerns, I would let it rest for now. They may not be ready to share. Instead, work on continuing to establish rapport. You can make some small talk, or move on to the next two questions, both of which should produce more positive feelings, and try again later if the moment seems right.

Wrapping Up

You've asked someone their concerns and better understand where they're coming from. Now let's turn to the next question, in which you're going to examine a prior success so that you can pave the way for your own negotiation success in the final chapter and beyond.

NINE

HOW HAVE YOU HANDLED THIS SUCCESSFULLY IN THE PAST?

Rachel and Nick, out of college for five years and dating for two, moved in together six months ago. At the beginning of their relationship, they'd spent a lot of time outdoors, hiking on weekends, and also in the kitchen cooking together. Each had never felt happier. They had lots of family similarities and views on what was important to them in life. Both felt they were moving toward marriage.

Rachel has a demanding public relations job, while Nick works as a freelance graphic designer with mostly regular hours. Prior to this job, Rachel had spent three years as a PR manager at an established beauty company with regular hours but seemingly no room to move up. Then she was offered the chance to work at an emerging cosmetics brand, with a promotion to senior PR manager. Rachel was excited to work at a new company and represent products she would actually use. But her new job quickly ate up most of her life. The company was expanding rapidly, with all the growing pains you'd expect: turnover, changes in strategy. On top of this, Rachel's manager left unexpectedly two weeks into her job, and she had to pick up extra responsibility while they searched for the replacement. She went from not traveling at all to traveling once a month for almost a week. But the cultural changes impacted Rachel most. Not only did she spend more hours in the office on weekdays, but her evenings and weekends became consumed by texts, calls, and requests to respond to the latest "fire drill." Her CEO was an eccentric personality who demanded immediate responses, sometimes contradicted herself, and occasionally yelled. Rachel often felt stressed. Even when the texts had seemed to stop for the evening, Rachel, fearing she might miss an alert, would continue to check her phone as she and Nick watched television.

Nick grew resentful of Rachel's lack of free time, frequently rolling his eyes and making cutting comments about her work. Each of them started to feel disconnected. Weekend activities slowed down and almost stopped. The last time they had gone hiking, they were in an area with spotty cell phone coverage, and Rachel spent most of the hike stressed that she might miss something. They drove home in silence.

Finally, Nick and Rachel sat down to talk things out. Nick felt Rachel had chosen her job over their relationship. Rachel told Nick she felt frustrated with his eye rolling, and also helpless, like he was blaming her for something she couldn't control. The work environment had been high pressure and relentless. Rachel, too, had felt desperate for more balance in her life.

Nick said, "I know you're wired differently from me. I need a lot of free time, and you've always liked working hard. How have you managed to have a life in your previous jobs?" Rachel thought back and told Nick about her first year out of college, when she worked on a U.S. presidential campaign as one of the coordinators for her home state. The hours were intense and the demands of the job seemingly endless. She had been in a relationship then, too, and struggled to find time to connect. But once she had acclimated and built credibility with her team, she'd found ways to set boundaries around some of her weekends and weeknights. She did this by looking in advance to see when important fund-raising deadlines or events were happening, and then finding other times that seemed likely to be slower. She worked with her interns to build their knowledge so that they could sub in for her sometimes. Then she communicated in advance when she needed time off and arranged for coverage. Now that she was thinking about it, Rachel remembered that she had even negotiated time every day when she could run or go to the gym and not be called except in real emergencies—and that had been a huge mood lifter. She realized she hadn't gone for a run in weeks.

As she talked, Rachel started to think out loud about how she could put this strategy into practice in her current job, now that she'd been there a year. Yes, there were times when she would have to work weekends. But not *every* weekend. As chaotic as things could be sometimes, she was starting to see a rhythm to things—like times around their events or investor calls where breaks might be possible. Plus, she was a senior manager now—and a great boss, someone who shared information and strategies with her team. She had a terrific PR manager below her who was asking for more responsibility. With a bit of training, this manager could cover for Rachel sometimes.

These ideas all helped Rachel to feel better about her current situation—and her relationship with Nick. But she also realized, in the process of detailing this prior success, that she was able to get through the demanding presidential campaign in part because she knew it was time-limited, and she had a supportive boss. This PR job had no time limit, and her boss didn't always communicate respectfully, or consistently. While Rachel wanted to work hard and advance in her career, she also needed time for her health, as well as the important people in her life. Recalling what had made her prior campaign job sustainable gave Rachel permission to consider whether this job was the best fit for her in the long term.

Rachel and Nick came out of this conversation with a plan. She would negotiate for her Saturdays and Sunday mornings off, unless there was an emergency. They would have two nights a week where she turned off her phone after seven p.m., so they could have dinner and talk. Nick in turn promised to show more support for what Rachel was going through at work, that if she indicated she was dealing with an emergency, Nick would empathize rather than blame—and curtail the eye rolls. And Rachel started a casual job search, remaining open to the possibility of either staying and continuing to negotiate for what she needed, or finding another challenging position that also offered a respectful and healthy work culture. The following weekend, they went for a Saturday hike and each felt like they could draw a deep breath for the first time in months.

Asking about a Prior Success

In this chapter, we once again travel back in time to help the other person remember ways in which they have successfully handled challenges similar to the one they—and you—face now.

We know from the Mirror section that asking yourself about a prior success yields all sorts of helpful benefits. It triggers our memory bank of experiences to allow us to expand our pie of potential options for our current situation by examining where we've had success previously. In addition, memory influences how we make decisions; it affects how we feel about the path ahead of us. Memory can influence our sense of motivation and empowerment, and help us solve our next issue.

In asking this question of someone else, you will open up a window so that you can expand your view of the other person and get to know more about what has made them successful in the past. You'll gather important data about what has worked for this person in the past, and what might work for them—and you—again in the future.

Additionally, in asking about a prior success, you'll anchor the other person in positive, empowering feelings that research has shown to improve the way they will handle their next interpersonal interaction—with you! In this chapter, I will give you strategies to put the other person back in a success mind frame so that they can access their inner wisdom and generate ideas that will help move them forward. And if they can't recall a previous similar success, I'll help you follow up with them to find a different kind of previous success; you will then work with them to find similarities to the current situation. Together, you'll leave this chapter empowered and ready to move toward what comes next.

Recalling a Prior Success Helps Someone Define Their Problem and Access Potential Solutions

When you ask someone this question, you allow them to remember and review, in detail if possible, the techniques and strategies that have worked for them in the past. When you help them remember what has worked in the past, you'll be better positioned to work with them to figure out which of those strategies will work for both of you in this negotiation.

Remember that in asking "How have you handled this successfully in the past?" you first need to understand what "this" is. "This" is your problem or goal from our first Window question, "Tell me." Which means we are going back to that answer to make sure we have accurately defined the problem or goal. In the example that started this chapter, Rachel and Nick both supported Rachel's need to work hard, and also desired to work on their partnership. Together, they defined the problem as "How can we honor Rachel's career ambition while also finding space to nourish our relationship?"

Once you know the goal you're working on, or the problem you are solving, recalling a prior related success helps you and the other person remember concrete strategies that might help again in your current negotiation. In many situations, this question will help you refine your understanding of the problem you want to solve and give you ideas to fix it.

Let's go back to Smith and Rosa, the contractor and homeowner who worked together successfully on a number of home improvement projects in Rosa's apartments up until their most recent job, which fell apart and resulted in litigation. Imagine that they sit down together to negotiate, and the mediator asks them: "Okay, so you both say your collaboration was great until this last job. How did you handle your previous work together so successfully?" The homeowner says, "Well, those were smaller jobs, and I also had more time to communicate with him on design choices. This time I had a lot going on, and he ended up picking those terrible cabinets." The contractor says, "Usually we had a written contract, and she had always paid me a twenty-five percent down payment upfront. This time, since we'd already done a number of jobs together, we just shook hands on it. But she never paid me that deposit—or anything, for that matter. I know she was taking her kid to college, but how does that justify completely missing the payment?"

Asking about a prior success gave us so much information, both to diagnose what happened here and to help these two people figure out how they might work together better in the future. These two entrepreneurs were the victims of their own prior success. Rather than being some terrible personality conflict, we now know that this conflict resulted because they (1) trusted each other enough not to have a contract, which ended up backfiring; (2) were working on a bigger job than they'd ever done together before; (3) had been unable to communicate about design choices due to outside commitments; and (4) hadn't followed their usual plan when it came to payment. Just in considering what made them successful in the past, we figured out that writing a contract with payment dates, and setting aside time for joint design choices, seemed to be their winning formula.

Recalling a Prior Success Acts as a Power Prime

The second reason to ask about a prior success is that it helps the other person gather the confidence and motivation to help solve the problem you both face. Remembering that feeling of power or confidence can help tremendously when facing a negotiation.

Research shows the value of what Columbia Business School professor Adam Galinsky and his co-authors call "power priming," or the act of "coax[ing] ourselves into feeling more or less powerful than we typically feel." Hundreds of studies have shown that simply recalling a previous time in which one had power can produce the same effects as actually having power in the present situation. Power priming can be especially helpful when we face challenging or stressful experiences, like in negotiation.

Recalling a prior success acts as a power prime. You used it yourself in chapter 4, and here, you're going to use that question to achieve a similar effect with someone else. You'll remind them of a time when things went well for them, so that they can place this current negotiation into context. Looking at a prior success will help them see themselves, and the current situation, more positively, which may help you generate solutions that will be more advantageous for you both.

Asking an Adversary about a Prior Success?

When I teach this question in workshops, people sometimes ask me: Do you really want to ask your adversary about a prior success? What if you're both trying to get as much as possible from the negotiation?

First, remember that your adversary during the negotiation is often your partner after the deal is done. Asking your boss for a better compensation package? Negotiating a good price and shelf space for your product at a large chain store? Trying to get another country to agree to the enforcement language you want in a joint resolution? Advocating for your client to upgrade to a package that better reflects the work they need you to do? Many of these situations require you to problem-solve with the other person at the table, or work with them again once this conversation is complete. Asking them how they have handled similar situations in the past successfully expands the pie of options so that you can better advocate for the ones that make sense for you.

Also, just because you're asking for their ideas doesn't mean you have to adopt all of them. Remember, you have already done the work to understand your own goals, needs, and ideas. So once you hear ideas from them, you'll be able to evaluate them against the backdrop of everything you uncovered in the Mirror section. All this question does is expand the universe of possible options that will also meet your needs. If they raise something that doesn't work for you, you'll be able to articulate exactly why, and offer alternatives.

And even if the person you're negotiating with is not someone with whom you will have an ongoing relationship, I've seen this question produce great results. If you're negotiating for a potential job, for example, and having a disagreement with the prospective hiring manager over salary, asking how they have successfully resolved a concern like this in the past may give you useful information. Maybe in the end they didn't offer enough salary to make the job work, but if they offered you a budget for training and personal development and that sounded appealing, you could ask your next prospective employer what they offer on that front.

Finally, asking an adversary about a prior success also has the benefit of establishing rapport. By treating the other person as a partner in your negotiation, you increase the odds that they will want to do something beneficial for you, too.

Your Turn in the Window: Asking about a Prior Success

Now that we know *why* this question is so beneficial, it's time to turn to the *how*: as we did for ourselves in the Mirror chapter, we are going to ask about a prior success. This time we're doing it through the Window, so that we can get a better view of the other person and what they are thinking.

Land the Plane

After you ask about a prior success, land the plane. As a reminder, that means that you ask this question and . . . that's it. Some examples we want to avoid: "How have you handled this successfully in the past? . . . What about last year's sales meeting?" or "From my perspective, you've been really successful at . . ."

Enjoy the Silence

After you ask the question, make room for the silence that may follow. Allow the person the time to sort through their mental Rolodex of prior situations and come up with a success that resonates for them. If they ask for help, then read on for how to help.

Follow Up

You want to follow up in a way that helps both of you get the most from this question. After asking about a prior success, you want to do for the other person what you did for yourself by allowing them to picture in as much detail as possible what the prior success looked and felt like. Remember how I had asked you to close your eyes and picture your previous success in as much detail as possible—what it felt, sounded, and tasted like? What posture or location were you in? I also asked you to remember the time leading up to that moment: your preparation, thoughts, tasks, and emotion.

You did this because the above is useful data—remembering everything that went into a prior success helps you prepare to repeat it. Plus, when you recall a previous success, research shows that you are more likely to perform better in your next negotiation. When I ask people about a previous success, I try to help them recall that success in as much vivid detail as possible, and you're also going to do that for someone else. How? You're going to use two key skills you've been practicing: following up and summarizing.

Revisit your notes on what the person told you about their previous success. You're going to ask about these one at a time, using "Tell me more . . ." For example: "Thanks for all this helpful information. Can you tell me more about the training and personal development budget?" Or, "Smith and Rosa, can you tell me more about the successful contracts you drafted in the past?" Then summarize: "It sounds like you pushed hard for this training budget and have been pleased that you got it through.

Most of your competitors don't have this, and you've found it to be successful in retaining and developing great talent." Or, "It sounds like you clearly spelled out payment amounts and dates, as well as some language around design choices."

Following Up if the Person Can't Recall a Similar Success

If the other person has trouble recalling a prior success—maybe saying to you, "This is the first time I have ever faced this issue"—then remember that you can still help them by asking them to recall a prior success that has any element similar to the current situation you're discussing. In this way, you can help the person you're talking to cast a wider net, and recall a prior success that may still give them useful data in solving the issue at hand.

Let's look at some examples to see how recalling a different, but related, success can work as a means of helping you through your negotiation. If you're working with your boss on an issue where a client who initially seemed happy is now questioning the entire project close to delivery, and this is the first time this has happened, you might ask them whether they'd ever had a last-minute success getting another working relationship back on track—with a coworker, for example. Perhaps there are techniques they used in that situation that could also work for a client-facing situation.

Or, imagine that Smith and Rosa, the contractor and homeowner, had never worked together before. You might ask them to recall a different but related success. For example, you might say to the contractor, "You've said you never worked with this homeowner before. How have you handled contracts successfully with other clients?" And to the homeowner, "You said you felt the design communication was lacking here—how have you handled this successfully with other contractors?"

Similarly, if your spouse is worried because you have a financial planning issue between you, and this is the first time you've faced that problem, you might ask, "How do you feel we have successfully handled other issues between us in the past?" This type of question will help them see beyond the recent, specific failure they are consumed with, and open up new sources of helpful information. Again, you'll want to follow up with a question about how they felt: "How did it feel when we were able to get through that problem and become close again?" This will help anchor the person in those positive feelings, which in turn will unlock their creativity to solve the new, and different, issue before them.

What if the person you're negotiating with is having trouble recalling any success at all? As you did with yourself, ask the other person about any area in which they have felt successful. One career coach I spoke with told me a story about a client of hers who was having great difficulty defining his goals for their work together. The client, who had been out of the workforce for a while and now wanted to get back to work, kept tossing out half-hearted (and often conflicting) ideas and then shooting them down, with the result that they weren't making much progress in their work together. The client had trouble even working on updating his résumé or attending a networking event. When the coach asked the client how he had successfully made career decisions in the past, he froze and said he didn't have any successes to speak of. He had basically graduated college, tried a few things briefly, and then took a break to parent his children.

The coach switched tacks and said, "No worries. That's why we're working together—to help jump-start you in this area. Where else in your life have you felt more successful?" The client sheepishly said, "Well, I guess I did lose seventy pounds . . . and I've managed to keep it off. Five years ago I found out I was prediabetic and decided to make a change." The coach reflected back this incredible accomplishment, and asked him more questions about actions he took to make himself successful. She watched as the client's confidence grew. Slowly, they started to make progress on his résumé and career objectives. This prior success, while unrelated to his career, still had the power to help this client negotiate his way toward his goals.

Summarize and Ask for Feedback

It's no surprise that most people love hearing about their successes, so when I reflect these back, I like to really show that I've heard all the details. So, as an example, let's take the situation where your boss is facing a major, last-minute client problem. You don't have a prior client example to examine, but your boss has told you about an internal situation that she handled under time pressure. Your summary could look something like, "Wow. I had no idea that you had handled such a major issue with [coworkers X and Y] until you told me about it just now. I guess that speaks to the success you had in resolving it—no one around here knew. So to sum it up, it wasn't a client-facing issue but an issue between two account executives about who would have which responsibilities on the account. And it came up last minute. It sounds like you resolved it by convening them together so that you could cut down on the email misunderstandings. And once they were in person, you helped them focus on their common objective—doing the best work possible for this client while also advancing their careers. You listened to their concerns so they felt confident they had been heard. And you asked for ideas. Ultimately, this conversation helped each of them feel good about what role they could play on this account, and you were able to go forward with the original division of labor."

In this way, you're able to help your boss feel good about her work on this issue—but you've also highlighted all the specific actions she took to make this situation successful. And bringing up those actions will help you greatly in moving to the next, and last, question—one in which you're looking to the future and trying to solve the client problem.

Wrap up your summary by asking for feedback, so that you can make sure you haven't missed anything. You might also find, as I frequently have, that when you summarize back their prior success, the other person might respond to add even more actions they took that contributed to their success. For example, your boss might say, "Yes, that's right—but now that I'm thinking about it, I think what also helped is that I followed up with each of the executives after our joint meeting, just to thank them for participating and helping me reach a resolution for this client. It created even more good feeling that helped us weather some stressful times down the road." In this way, you've made the other person feel great, and generated even more ideas that may help make you successful in this negotiation.

Listen for What Is Not Said

Finally, you'll want to make sure you pay attention to any body language you see when you ask this question. It's most helpful to notice any changes from someone's baseline, or default posture, expression, or tone of voice. If someone's body language baseline appears to be that they tend to lean away from you when you're negotiating, and all of a sudden they sit up, or even lean in, that may be a sign that you're having a positive effect in engaging them. The tone of their voice may rise. They may smile more, or open their eyes wider. Remember that a lot of our communication is non-verbal, and if you're picking up on those cues, you'll take much more from this question—and the rest of the Window questions—that will help you in your negotiation.

Wrapping Up

You've just helped someone discuss a prior success that likely gave you clues to help solve the challenge before you now. In the last question, you'll put everything together and start to look to the future. At the end of this next chapter, you'll be ready to launch yourself into the future with the best possible chance of success.

TEN

WHAT'S THE FIRST STEP?

In just two years, David Greenwald led his firm—Fried, Frank, Harris, Shriver & Jacobson LLP ("Fried Frank")—from the bottom 2 percent to the top 10 percent in a key employee satisfaction metric—while increasing productivity and hours worked. And it all started with one unexpected step.

When David joined Fried Frank, an international law firm, as its chairman late in 2013, he found a number of pressing issues before him. David told me, "Our revenues were down, and our profits down even more. We'd just finished an especially poor year for the firm in terms of our financial results. And it wasn't just that one year. When I looked back a decade or more, and compared us to our peers and how they'd grown, it was clear that Fried Frank had fallen behind."

Another major issue? His associate satisfaction ranking was in the basement. When law firms refer to an associate, they are talking about a lawyer who isn't a partner, or owner, of the firm. At a large firm like Fried Frank, associates comprise the majority of the firm's lawyers, in many cases outnumbering partners by 4 to 1 or more. Which means that if many of the associates are unhappy, a large portion of your entire firm is unhappy.

Every year, a publication called *The American Lawyer* ranks the nation's biggest law firms on a number of metrics, one being the satisfaction of their mid-level associates—those lawyers who are in their third, fourth, or fifth year of practice. The overall satisfaction ranking takes into account things like the associates' satisfaction with work, benefits and compensation, partner-associate relations, training and guidance, management's openness about firm strategies and partnership chances, the firm's attitude toward pro bono work and billable hours, and the likelihood of the associate being at the firm in two years.

In 2013, out of the nation's 134 large law firms that were ranked in the survey, Fried Frank's associate satisfaction ranking was 132.

David told me, "I went into our next partnership meeting and said, 'Well, the first piece of good news is we don't have far to fall. The second piece of good news is that we have a lot of room to move up.'"

Looking around the firm, David could see Fried Frank's associate satisfaction problem reflected in more than just this ranking. "The low morale showed up in a couple of ways. One, we had high turnover. Now, law firms generally have a lot of turnover, and some of that is expected—but the issue is, where are those people going? And why are they going? We had people leaving us unhappy. And they weren't going home to Chicago, where we don't have an office, or to a different kind of legal job, like a corporation. They were going to our peer firms. In other words, these were people who wanted to practice law in a big firm—just not at Fried Frank. And we needed to change that." David also looked at their recruiting numbers and felt that Fried Frank was not doing nearly as well as it should.

After spending some time getting a handle on the firm's issues, David set about to change the culture around the way associates and partners communicated. And he did it from the top. Starting in early 2015, he established twice-yearly town hall meetings where he would speak to all the associates about substantive matters, including firm strategy. He also met regularly with a smaller associate committee. And one of the first things he did in those meetings? He asked them what steps he could take to make things better. In spring 2015, after David met with his associates and asked for their ideas, *The American Lawyer* surveyed associates again about their satisfaction with Fried Frank. Fried Frank's satisfaction ranking jumped from its sub-100 position to #16 out of 101.

Then, the associates came up with an idea. And it wasn't at all what David expected. For years, the associates said they had been asking for an associates-only lounge in their New York headquarters, a place where they could gather to talk, work, or just relax while they were in the office. Their request had gone nowhere. David jumped on the opportunity. The associates made the request for the lounge on September 15, 2015. The partnership approved it almost immediately, announced to the firm by Thanksgiving, and then opened it a few months later, in February.

What's in the associates' lounge? A foosball table, ping-pong table, a large TV, soft furniture for relaxing, as well as snacks and drinks. But what it meant to the associates was much greater. David told me, "What that lounge did for our relationship with the associates was huge. As a partnership, it gave us credibility—they asked for something and we got it done, quickly. It helped us build trust. And it also elevated the level of our discussions more generally. Before, I think the associates were used to feeling ignored, so they didn't ask us questions about substantive matters. But now we talk about everything: our international strategy, financial performance, diversity, the review process. Once they knew their views would be considered, they started asking terrific questions and engaging with us."

David goes on: "Our associates are the future of the firm. They're the vast majority of lawyers at the firm. One day, one of them will have my job. And so they're very important. We want and need them to be motivated and happy. The lounge was a great first step toward that goal."

In spring 2016, *The American Lawyer* surveyed associates again about their satisfaction with Fried Frank. Fried Frank's satisfaction ranking catapulted into the top ten, landing them at #8.

What was even more remarkable: the associates were more satis-fied while also working more hours. Between 2013, the year Fried Frank scraped the bottom of the barrel at #132, and 2016, when they ranked #8 out of #94, the number of hours worked by their associates *increased* by more than 10 percent. And the firm's financial results have turned around, too. In 2018, for the first time in the firm's history, Fried Frank passed the $3 million mark in profits per equity partner (PEP); that number repre-sented 100 percent growth from where they were in 2013.

Recently, a reporter visited David to interview him about Fried Frank's transformation. The reporter asked to see the associates' lounge. David told him, "Well, we can see it if you want. But I can't get us in. My access card doesn't work." Incredulous, the reporter replied, "You're the chairman, can't you open any door at the firm?" David explained that the associates had wanted a place that was just for them. Together, they walked down the hall and tried David's access card. It was denied. He had kept to his word.

Your Turn in the Window

So far in your negotiation, you've covered a lot of ground: You've asked the other person their view of the situation, you've delved into their con-cerns and needs, and you've also asked them what those needs would look like. You've covered how they have handled an issue like this successfully in the past, and gathered some useful information. This is your last chance to look through the Window and see them, and your situation, as clearly as possible. Now you will have the chance to ask them to look forward, just as you've done.

At this stage, asking "What's the first step?" is important for many rea-sons. This question benefits your deal, helping you generate as many op-tions as possible for a solution to your negotiation. Again, listening to the other side doesn't mean you need to accept everything you hear. But by asking you increase the chance that some option they offer, or a variation on that option, will also meet the needs you unearthed in the Mirror section.

Next, this question benefits the negotiators—both you and the other person—in several ways. When you ask someone their ideas for a first step, you treat them as a partner in your negotiation, making it more likely they will accord your ideas the same listening and respect you showed theirs. We know from psychology professor Robert Cialdini that people tend to reciprocate gestures in negotiation, meaning that if you do something for someone, you're more likely to get them to do it for you in response. Asking someone else for their ideas, especially a coworker or loved one, also gives them the chance to demonstrate leadership and connects them to a sense of purpose, which makes them happier in whatever work they're doing—in the office or at home. And research shows that by asking other people questions about their ideas, you cultivate what Stanford psychologist Carol Dweck calls a "growth mind-set" that helps you learn and achieve more.

Finally, asking for the first step is important because it can establish momentum, and a path forward, even if you don't yet know all the steps you want to take.

Asking the First Step Benefits the Deal

In negotiation, one of our goals is to generate as many ideas as possible, in hopes of reaching the idea that will allow us to achieve our objectives. Those who are in scientific fields know that it often takes many ideas— and many unsuccessful ideas—to find one that makes people's lives better. John Kirwan, a rheumatology professor at the University of Bristol, embarked on a study to find out exactly what percentage of his ideas were successful over the course of his twenty-three years in practice. He had had a lot of success for a medical academic, with many works published and cited within his field. Nonetheless, many of his ideas failed. His study revealed that 75 percent of the 185 ideas he found in his archives led to no publications. By his own assessment, only 2.7 percent of his ideas met his criteria to be considered "especially good." The professor told *Quartz* magazine that despite this number, he considered all the failed ideas to have great value: "The issue here is to recognize that in science (and indeed, perhaps in life as a whole) we have lots of ideas that don't work out. You cannot tell initially if the idea will work or not—you need to explore it and do some work on it in order to find out. This is a necessary process . . . we are not wasting our time in exploring ideas that turn out not to work—we are helping to generate good ideas."

No matter how many innovative ideas we generate on our own, we can't assume we know what our negotiation partner thinks about the future, or what ideas they may have. Like in the example of David and Fried Frank above, you might find an idea that meets someone else's needs while also meeting yours. Some parents I know who have negotiated with their kids over screen use report that their kids have come up with creative ideas, such as setting technology-free zones in the house (like bedrooms and the dining room table), starting "screen-free Saturdays" where the family does an outdoor activity together, or establishing a chore or homework chart to earn time.

Even where one side in the negotiation has most or all the expertise needed to come up with a universe of potential options, inviting the other person to contribute can yield benefits for the long-term success of the deal. For example, recent research and teaching shows that when doctors consult with patients on treatment options, it improves patient compliance with treatment as well as health outcomes. In a *New York Times* article, "Teaching Doctors the Art of Negotiation," Dr. Dhruv Khullar said, "The medical profession is no longer one in which doctors dictate a given treatment course to patients, who are then expected to follow it. Rather, clinicians and patients deliberate about treatment options, weigh costs and benefits together, and determine the best course of action." When doctors consult with patients on what steps to take, patients not only feel more satisfaction with the doctor, but are more likely to stick with their decided treatment path, resulting in better outcomes and lower healthcare costs.

Finally, asking someone to contribute future-focused ideas in negotiation can help with counterpunchers—the term I use for someone who shoots down your ideas without contributing any of their own. Asking this question invites them to participate more productively in the search for a solution.

Asking the First Step Benefits the Negotiators

Asking the first step also benefits the people in your negotiation. Partnering with someone else in decision-making leads not only to short-term benefits (for example, the idea for an associates' lounge that costs little and buoys morale) but long-term benefits as well (happier and more engaged associates who have partnered with you in thinking through and solving challenging issues).

Even where one person has more subject matter expertise in the negotiation, asking the other person their preferred first step can yield benefits for both parties in the negotiation. Let's revisit our doctor and patient example. Medical research shows that by presenting the list of possible options to the patient and asking for their thoughts, you benefit both parties in the doctor-patient relationship by increasing the patient's adherence to whatever treatment option is selected. When patients stick to their treatment plan, the patient saves money associated with relapse and collateral consequences, and the doctor improves statistics while creating savings for the hospital and insurers. In a time when patient noncompliance with treatment is estimated to cost billions of dollars, asking the patient to participate in deciding the course of treatment produces profound benefits for both parties in that negotiation.

Finally, asking someone else for their ideas on first steps benefits the negotiators by benefiting their relationship. This is true not only at work, where people thrive on a feeling of connection with their coworkers, but in relationships outside the workplace. More than ever before, experts are studying what leads to healthy personal relationships, and the answers include qualities like empathy, responsiveness to partners' concerns, and trust. You increase all those qualities when you ask someone else for their ideas and sincerely listen to their answers.

Asking an Adversary for Ideas?

When thinking about your approach to a negotiation, it always makes sense to consider to what extent you will need to work with this person once your negotiation is done. Most industries, no matter how large, can end up feeling more like a neighborhood, especially at the top. Gabriel Matus, general counsel of Excel Sports Management, a premier sports agency, told me, "Our industry is surprisingly small. When you manage high-caliber athletes, you see the same people over and over again. In professional services like this, it's important to maintain good relationships."

Asking the other person for their ideas is a sign of respect and collaboration. It's the final step in building a foundation of trust upon which long, productive, and lucrative partnerships are built. It lets them know that you are interested in them, whether personally or professionally.

Bottom line: asking people for their ideas in negotiation usually costs you nothing, and can benefit you greatly.

One Step at a Time to Solve Problems

Asking for one step can lead to a more comprehensive solution to all the issues on the table. Even if your conversation yields a bunch of ideas, you may want to start in one place, as David did with the associates' lounge. He knew that that one step would have symbolic benefits that went far beyond simply establishing a place for associates to hang out. It was a physical, tangible reminder that the firm listened to them, and valued what they had to say.

But sometimes you need to take solutions one step at a time. Perhaps only one step is feasible at the moment, or there's one you may want or need to try first before moving on to the others.

For example: Jamie, a Division I college basketball player with serious back problems—a possible herniated disc that wasn't getting better with rest—went to the Mayo Clinic for evaluation. She, the doctor, and her family knew there were a couple of possible solutions: they could try the conservative route and do physical therapy, or opt for surgery. The doctor asked the patient and her family what they wanted to do for their first step. Jamie, a sophomore, decided she wanted to try and finish out her sophomore basketball season. She felt that the conservative approach would allow her to do that and also give her the peace of mind to know that they had tried everything before surgery. The doctor supported that choice. Jamie committed to working hard in physical therapy and was able to finish out the year. "I played through the season, and it went relatively well. I had back pain, but I was able to manage it enough to where I could play. The physical therapy really helped me," she later told the Mayo Clinic. At the end of the season, and after an MRI showed no change in her condition, Jamie opted for the surgery. The physical therapy had helped, but didn't eliminate her chronic pain. Having taken the conservative first step helped Jamie and her family feel good about knowing the next step to take. The surgery was successful and Jamie returned to the court in the fall.

And sometimes, one step saves lives. About ten years ago, two women accompanied me into a small room in the Bronx and seated themselves on opposite sides of the table. They were residents of the same apartment complex, and ongoing tension between them had spilled over into physical fights. Tension had built to the point where their families, their pastor, and even the police, who had been called to the scene several times, recommended mediation because they were concerned about the prospect of major violence.

Once seated, the women spoke bravely and candidly about what would happen if they continued on their current path of conflict. One said to the other, "You know, I could hurt you. I've thought about that. But I'd go to jail. My kids would get taken away, and I don't have any relatives to take them. They'd go into foster care, and that's not happening. So we need another way." It became evident that there would be no reconciliation, no best friendship or happy embrace. But we asked each of the women to think about what could be their first step toward a future that did not include police involvement or prison time. They considered the question and agreed not to harm each other. We closed the mediation with a prayer from their pastor. Their journey started with one critical, life-changing step.

Now for the "How"

How do you ask this question effectively? Here are some ways you might formulate this question without narrowing or changing it:

- What's our first step?
- What do you see as our first step here?

If you're communicating productively with the other side, or have the sense that you may be able to take more than one step, you might try:

- What ideas do you have for the future?
- What are your thoughts on how we can move forward?

In the last sections of this chapter, I'm going to give you some tips to help you ask this question with the greatest success, and then troubleshoot a few issues that might arise.

Land the Plane

You've just asked someone for their ideas. Now wait to hear their answers. This question may yield unexpected and beneficial solutions for you and the other person.

Enjoy the Silence

This is a big question. You are asking the other person to participate with you in designing your future. They may have done their homework already, and have ideas at the ready. Or they may need time. And when I say time, I mean more than two seconds. This is where I have seen many negotiators falter. They ask the question, wait two seconds, and then ask another question, or fill in their own ideas. Example: "What ideas do you have to move forward? . . . Should we start with the salary piece?" Resist! Even if you're just tacking on another question, you're cutting off the discussion and biasing the result. You'll know if the other person needs help if they ask you for help. Otherwise, stay quiet.

Follow Up

If the other person gives you an idea and you need to understand more about it, "Tell me more . . ." is a great place to start. If the idea is vague, or you're not sure how to put it into practice—for example, the person says, "I want us to communicate better with our clients"—you could return to the follow-up question from chapter 7 ("What do you need?") and ask them in response, "What would communicating better with our clients look like?"

And what if you're dealing with someone who suggests something . . . unproductive? I once heard about a high-profile legal negotiation in which one of the parties, when asked for settlement ideas, said, "I have an idea. You can _____ my _____." I won't fill in the blanks, but suffice it to say he did not suggest that the other person read his proposal or water his plants. This has happened to me more than once. I mediate cases in New York City, where sometimes idle threats are just another day at the office. I once asked a party in Small Claims Court what our first step should be, and in front of the other party, he said, "I'll give you an idea. I could Taser the ____ out of him!"

I hope you don't find yourself in this situation, but if you do, here is my suggestion for how to handle it. I simply ask something like, "How does [Tasering him] help us achieve our goals here today?" If I've been listening to them, I already know their goals, needs, and concerns. So I can simply repeat what they've told me they need, and ask how this new idea will help them achieve it. For example, if they have told me they need to move on with their life, I might say, "You've told me your goal here is to settle this so that you can move on with your life. How does Tasering him help you achieve that?"

Sometimes, this follow-up question is enough to produce a more helpful response. If that doesn't help, I suggest taking a break until we can have more productive discussions.

Summarize and Ask for Feedback

Again, you'll want to summarize what you hear and ask for feedback. Sometimes in the process of hearing their ideas repeated back to them, people may come to reflect on them and make changes. Hearing David's summary of the associate lounge plans helped encourage additional problem-solving—and, in turn, helped create a culture of collaboration.

Listen for What Is Not Said

As always, you'll want to be attentive to any non-verbal communication you see during this question. For example, "Correct me if I'm wrong, but it seemed as though you looked doubtful when I asked for your ideas. You may be wondering if I'm sincere in wanting to hear them. I know we haven't always communicated that well in the past, but I'd like to change that. Your ideas are important. I can't promise I'll agree with everything you say, but I absolutely promise to listen."

Troubleshooting

Now that we've gone through how to ask this question, let's talk about how to tackle a few issues you might occasionally face in asking it.

How Do You Generate Ideas if This Is a Group Negotiation?

If you're working on a group negotiation, whether it's among family, colleagues, or nations, you may want to be more deliberate about how you generate ideas than simply asking someone on the spot. For many years, people thought that group brainstorming, a process in which people would get together and shout out as many ideas as came to mind, would produce the best, most innovative results. More recent research, however, shows that group brainstorming often doesn't work because it can produce shallow or flashy ideas that often don't hold up under further testing, especially for important or challenging problem-solving. You may want to give people some time to think and then come back with their ideas. Individual work that then gets honed in a group is a much better way to generate ideas. When I help people design their first step in a negotiation, I usually ask them each individually to generate some ideas before we come together and evaluate them.

So what does that mean for this question? The good news is that you're already ahead of many people who come into a negotiation having waited until the group session to start generating their ideas. You've already started thinking about possible first steps to take. You've done your homework. You're now asking other people to do the same individual work you did by inviting them to discuss possible first steps. You may just want to allow them some reflection time to do the same work you did.

What If the Other Person Isn't Ready?

Be prepared that the other person may not be ready for this question at the moment you ask it. They may want some time to digest the information that came out of the four Window questions you asked and the answers you summarized. If that's the case, you might ask them for another meeting when they're ready to discuss, or share with them some of the ideas you generated, and then ask for a follow-up conversation to hear their thoughts.

What if the Next Step Seems Automatic?

And what about the opposite scenario, in which the next step seems automatic, or baked into the process? For example, you've just finished an introductory interview with HR and you've been told the next step is a call-back interview with management. I would still ask, "What more can you tell me about our next steps?" You might be surprised at the additional information you gain, perhaps about the timing of those steps, who the decision-makers will be, or even the likelihood of your application moving forward. Asking the question also makes you look motivated and organized. Bottom line: it's always better to try for more information.

What If You're the Junior Person in This Negotiation?

What if you are the more junior person in a boss-subordinate situation in which you are expected professionally to have formulated a plan forward? What if your manager actually turns the question around on you and says, "What's the first step? Well, shouldn't you be telling me?" As you've done with the previous four questions, you know the first thing you do after the other person speaks is to summarize before you follow up. So here, that might look something like, "Right, you'd like my thoughts. I anticipated that, and so I spent time before this meeting thinking about possible next steps. I have several ideas that I'd be happy to lay out. Or you could share some initial thoughts, so that my ideas will be more responsive. Your choice."

What If They Can't Think of Anything?

And what if the other person draws a blank when you ask them about a first step? Here are a couple of things I sometimes try. First, if I'm in a position of trust with this other person, I may want to know more about the roadblock so I can help. I might ask, "What makes this question feel challenging to answer?" Giving them the opportunity to talk through their barriers may end up revealing some good ideas.

And remember, when in doubt, you can always try thinking of the "worst idea." Tell the other person you have a trick that has helped you generate ideas in the past, and then ask them, "What's the worst step you/ we could take?" Sometimes, knowing what won't work gives you excellent clues as to what will.

Wrapping Up

Congratulations! You've finished all ten questions. You've amassed more information than almost any other negotiator out there. And in the process of doing so, you may have even discovered a solution to your negotiation. Now you're ready to bring it home.

BRING IT HOME: CONCLUDING YOUR NEGOTIATION

Congratulations! You've finished *Ask for More*. By this point, you've asked yourself five open questions, listened to the answers, and summarized the internal wisdom you uncovered. You then asked someone else—perhaps a client, friend, spouse, or coworker—five open questions that uncovered a universe of new information. You listened, gave the person room to speak, followed up, and summarized. You worked through roadblocks and steered a relationship forward. You're in a great place compared to most negotiators—and compared to where you started.

You may be wondering: "Okay, I've asked the questions. What now?" Now is when you take the next step toward steering your future. The information you've learned in *Ask for More* will help you in any negotiation, whether you're looking to make a deal, pitch a client, resolve a relationship issue, settle a litigation, or reach a personal career goal.

I wrote this book because I know that asking questions is the best way to create a lifetime of value from every negotiation. But I also wrote it because by listening first, to yourself and then someone else, you equip yourself to *ask for more*—of yourself and others. I want you to use the tools contained in this book to *ask audaciously* for what you need, what you dream, what you know will create value for you as well as someone else. How to do that? Read on.

Sorting the Information You've Gathered

Ask for More helps you ask the right questions in order to explore the past, make sense of the present, and design a better future in negotiation. Each of the ten questions has a purpose. Now that you've completed all of them, the picture in front of you starts to look like this:

MIRROR	WINDOW
My definition of the problem/goal	Their definition of the problem/goal
My needs/what those look like	Their needs/what those look like
My feelings/concerns	Their feelings/concerns
My previous success	Their previous success
My first steps	Their first steps

A chart like this can be a helpful place for you to put down the summaries you did at the end of each chapter, or any other information you think might be helpful. I've included this as a handout at the end of this book (it's also available for download at my website, alexcarterasks .com/readerworksheet).

A lot of us are visual thinkers. Therefore, having a copy of this handout could be useful to actually have in front of you to fill out as you're negotiating. If you're in a close relationship with the other person at the table, or you're trying to build trust after a difficult situation, you might even consider showing them the questions and letting them know that you're trying a new approach to this conversation. For some people, that very act of transparency itself—visibly sharing your notes and working things out right in front of them—could be an important step toward building trust and moving forward.

Use These Questions to Set Successful Aspirations

We know that negotiators who go into negotiation focused on aspirations tend to be more successful than people who focus on what they can lose. Here's how you can use the questions and answers in this book to make sure you set your aspirations in the right place.

First, we know that aspirations are based on our needs. At the end of the Mirror section in chapter 5 ("What's the First Step?"), I asked you to look at your needs from chapter 2 ("What Do I Need?") and consider which steps would *fully and completely* satisfy your needs. Now that you're taking another look at these two answers together, do your steps from chapter 5 fully and completely satisfy your needs? If not, add more or make them higher.

Next, you'll need to make sure your aspirations are justifiable—and here's where the Window questions can help. Where possible, you'll want to tie your asks to anything objective you can find—for example, looking at comparable homes before you make an offer, or examining the costs of operating your business before setting prices for your products. But looking at the other person's answers to the five Window questions—their definition of the problem, their needs, emotions, successes, and ideas for the future—also tells you how the other person will think about your proposals. Make sure that your asks, while ambitious, can also be justified under at least one of those answers. If your goal is to raise your compensation by 20 percent, and your boss's primary goal is to reduce cash burn as much as possible right now while the company is trying to raise money, then you may face hurdles unless you can point to another need that would be satisfied by raising your pay (like reducing turnover), or show him ways in which raising your compensation could be compatible with that short-term financial goal (like hiring fewer staff in a less-needed position or increasing your equity, which gets paid out later).

Framing Your End of the Conversation

Once you have figured out your thoughts and goals, you'll want to frame them for maximum success.

What does "framing" mean? When you frame your thoughts, you're using a skill that many photographers and artists have used to great success. You're painting an image with your words that will resonate specifically with the person who's seeing it. And you can't frame for your audience unless you have a sense of what kinds of themes, words, and ideas will strike the right chord.

In other words, you can't persuade unless you listen first.

Framing is essential. Every negotiator should know and master this critical skill. If you're making an argument for why your department's budget should be increased, and you appeal to your manager's sense of equity across departments, that's not going to land if what she's really concerned about is the expected return on investment. If you're working to convince your child that he should try a new activity where he may not know anyone, persuading him that he can make new friends will not work if what he is concerned about is looking silly when trying something for the first time.

Briefly, here are three winning strategies for framing in negotiation:

First, where possible, frame your proposals in such a way that they actually respond to the other person's definition of the problem, needs, concerns, and ideas, as well as your own. For example, if you're looking to win a home renovation project and convince the homeowners to pay more for your proposal than their lower competing bid, you'll want to pick up on their needs for quality, dependability, and durability and let them know how you will meet those needs. If you're looking to reduce your children's evening screen time, you could let them know you've heard that they are tired in the mornings, and turning off the screens at night will help them feel better as they start their day. Having listened to the other person, you now understand much better how they process information and can pitch your proposals in the best possible way.

Second, focus people on what they can *gain* rather than what they *lose*. Studies show that human beings are very loss-avoidant, meaning that we want to avoid a loss even more than we want to achieve a gain—and that focusing on losses can reduce the other person's flexibility and willingness to compromise in negotiation. So for example, instead of saying to two of your employees, "I know you're best friends but I need to seat you two apart because I'm trying to reduce the cliques in our office," you instead could point out, "Each of you has told me you'd like to get to know more people in the department so you can advance in your careers. I've chosen seats for you that will allow you to work with some new people who will be important to your future promotion." Both of these statements are true. One of them is likely to move you back, and the other to move you forward.

Finally, be truthful, clear, and direct. When framing an argument, you want to put your best foot forward, but you also need to be consistent with the facts and situation. Framing involves directing people's attention to the portion of that picture you want to emphasize. But that doesn't mean showing people a picture of the White House and telling people they're looking at the Pyramids of Giza.

Being clear and direct is the best and also the most compassionate way to steer a relationship. A lot of times we mess up conversations by obfuscating how we really feel, or what we really want. Instead of saying, for example, "I feel really defensive when we talk about my spending," we cover up and play offense: "Well, it's pretty rich that you're talking to me about my spending when *you're* the one who suggested we take a vacation . . ." This leads to emotional escalation without getting to the heart of things. The direct route—i.e., stating what you actually mean—usually works best.

Transparency creates trust. That's the magic of the Mirror and the Window, right? You can see yourself and someone else more clearly. When you see clearly, you can speak more clearly. In doing so, you give the person a window into you, too. And you help them understand your proposals better, giving you the best chance for success.

Timing the Rest of Your Negotiation

So do you make that pitch or proposal on the spot, immediately after working through the questions? Part of determining whether to go forward includes an analysis of things like how much time you have. If this is a rare and precious opportunity, you might want to try to move forward right then and there. I might try to bargain for even a short break to gather your thoughts and organize yourself.

If you're dealing with someone in a long-term relationship, like a coworker, repeat client, or spouse—and you don't have immediate time pressure—just completing the questions, and obtaining all the data they yield, is enough of a success for one meeting. In fact, you might well want to take time to digest the information you learned and consider your path forward. You could, for example, thank the person for meeting you and sharing more of their concerns. Tell them how much you appreciate this and how it's given you food for thought. Then set another meeting time and use the information you learned to create a path forward.

In deciding whether to go forward or take a break, you should also consider whether you're the type of person who synthesizes things quickly, or whether you need time for reflection before making your next move. And the same is true for the other person in your negotiation. I have worked for both kinds of bosses, one who always said, "Let's do this!" and one who said, "Thanks for presenting this information, Alex. Let's set up a time to talk next week." Knowing this about yourself and the other person will help you make the decision that sets you up for the greatest success.

You also want to check the other person for signs of fatigue or emotional exhaustion. How long did your conversation last? What kind of topics came up? What was their reaction to these questions, and how did they seem to feel by the end of the conversation? Are they energized, asking, "So what's next?" Or do they show signs of fatigue? If they are tapping their watch or lapsing into checking email, that might be a sign that the stress of having been away from work for a bit is creeping up, and you'll want to set another time to make your ask. You want their full attention.

Also, make sure to check yourself for fatigue and emotional exhaustion. Listening like this takes a lot of focus. Depending on how long your conversation lasted and what emotions came up, you may need a break before moving forward. Sometimes my mediations with my students last a full day. When they do, we usually structure the day so that we spend the morning talking about the past and the afternoon talking about the future. And what do we do in the middle? We eat lunch. A break helps all of us regain focus and energy to start problem-solving.

If you do decide to reconvene at a later time, here's what you do to close the meeting. First, start with a summary of the progress you made and the information you shared. Next, thank the person for their time, energy, and openness. If any of you has made promises about doing any work—gathering information or documents, for example—between now and the next meeting, summarize that, too.

Where to Start the Discussion

So let's say you've decided to go forward after finishing these questions. After you ask your Window questions and summarize, the other person may open up and ask you some of the same questions. For example, they may ask you for your needs after you've asked theirs. If they do, you'll be prepared. If they don't ask you questions and instead seem ready to start talking about the future, you can let them know that you've prepared for this conversation so your thoughts and proposals would come from an informed place. You can then share as much of your answers as you like, and use them to frame any proposals you have.

When you craft your proposals, you have a wealth of information to help you do so more successfully. You might, for example, look at where their needs (chapter 7, "What Do You Need?") match up with yours (chapter 2, "What Do I Need?") and use that to design a solution that works for both parties. You can also look at how your vision for the future (chapter 5, "What's the First Step?") aligns or complements theirs (chapter 10, "What's the First Step?") in deciding what is likely to satisfy each of you. And if you know how they're feeling (chapter 8, "What Are Your Concerns?"), you can consider your own feelings (chapter 3, "What Do I Feel?") and consider how to frame your proposal in a way that maximizes your chances for success.

If your conversation brought up multiple issues, which do you tackle first? Here are some ideas:

LOW-HANGING FRUIT. If you share any common first steps, that's great! If you both agreed on something, summarize that and maybe propose it. Or if there's an issue on which you're pretty close, you might try narrowing the gap there and generating some momentum.

In fact, when I'm helping people negotiate, I often build a chart in my notes that looks something like this:

PERSON 1	COMMON	PERSON 2
Definition of the problem/goal		Definition of the problem/goal
Needs/what those look like		Needs/what those look like
Feelings/concerns		Feelings/concerns
Previous success		Previous success
First steps		First steps

The center column is where I put down any common information I hear. If the two negotiators agree on any first steps, that can be a great place to start and build momentum.

NEEDS OR FEELINGS IN COMMON. If both of you had one of the same needs or feelings, that too could be a great place to start. You can capture common feelings or concerns in the chart above and start there when finding a path forward.

Things to watch for and highlight: when you have common interests, feelings, or ideas about the problem but different visions for what to do about them. For example, both you and your department head are concerned that you're losing employees to a competitor. You think that one step toward retaining employees would be to offer more remote work, while your department head says, "Nothing short of more compensation is going to be effective." I find it helpful to summarize the common feeling or need, and the different options to meet it. You might decide together to generate some additional ideas (and/or survey employees on what they need) and strategize your solution.

SHORT-TERM ISSUES. If this is an ongoing negotiation or relationship, you might try something out for a few weeks or months and then set a second date to evaluate the approach and see how it went. For example, if you're working on communicating better with your partner about when you each need time off from childcare, it may be very helpful to try one approach—a schedule, trade, or even a secret hand signal—and set a time to meet again and talk about how it went. If you're negotiating with a new product distributor about inventory or shelf placement, you might have more success getting a short-term agreement and then trusting that the quality of your product will resonate with consumers.

RECURRING THEMES. If one need or feeling comes up over and over, you might need to work on that before anything else. Try tackling that one and then sequence others later. For example, if your department at work is divided over whether to hire a particular person, and the hiring process has left both sides feeling unheard and left out, you might need to address questions about the process first, before moving to discuss whether to hire. If you're working with a client on a large web design project and they keep talking about what they see as the lack of communication coming from your firm, you may want to talk about communication first before talking about the substance of the project.

Troubleshooting

As always, here is some advice for any snags you might encounter as you prepare to finish your negotiation.

What If Open Questions Don't Work?

Sometimes people aren't ready to open up when asked an open question. In that case, try to make a connection and find another way in. I'll never forget the time I took my student, Nona, to mediate a school absence case in New York City between a mom and a teenage son. The mom desperately wanted her son to go to school. The son had been absent to the point where his graduation could be in jeopardy. We sat down in mediation. My student asked the son many open questions, but got nothing but a shrug in return. Not a single word.

Finally, she asked the mom if we could talk to her son alone. The mom immediately packed up and said, "Great, you talk to him! Maybe he'll actually say something to you!" Then she left us in the room alone with him. My student mediator once again asked him open questions. Nothing.

Finally, she turned her chair away from me, and toward him. She leaned in and asked, "So, you're basically here 'cause you're forced to be, huh?" Not an open question. But it worked. He looked up, finally, and then shrugged again. But now she had his interest. She continued, "Me too. That's my professor over there (points at me). She says if I don't show up here every week, I fail the course." Brilliant move. The teenager opened up and started talking. When the open questions failed, she found a point of connection and used it to open the door. If you run into a similar roadblock, put these questions to the side. Try to make a human connection with the person across the table. Build some trust. You can always come back to these questions when you're both ready.

"Why Are You Talking Like This?"

My husband and I started dating after I'd learned the kind of listening we talk about in this book. But what about your relationships where the other person is, ahem, going to notice that you are not exactly talking like yourself? If the person reacts to your new open steering style with a "What have you been drinking?" or a slow blink of disbelief . . . that's fine! My advice: Be honest. Tell your loved one what you're doing and how it will help them as well as you. One way to respond could be: "You're absolutely right—this isn't the way I normally talk. I've been working on my communication, and listening better to the people around me. I'm going to be trying this from now on." For the workplace, you might try something like, "I've been studying negotiation and what people can do to create better conversations in the workplace. This conversation is important, and I wanted to approach it in the best way for both of us."

What If It Doesn't Work—At All?

And what if you're in a situation where these questions can't get you to your goal? I once had a student in my mediation class who, near the end of the semester, wrote me a weekly journal with a cover note that said, "Here is my weekly journal. Sorry if this is too personal." By now, I know that means, "Here's the real reason I took your class." In her journal, she talked about having a mother with Narcissistic Personality Disorder. She had enrolled in the Mediation Clinic in part because she wanted to learn a skill that might help her in her legal career—but really, what she wanted was to find a way to heal her relationship with her mother. She told me that the open questions and summarizing skills she had learned had been hugely helpful in clarifying her own goals and keeping their interactions more safe, but that she ultimately had not made progress with her mother, who continued to move the goalposts every time my student identified a common need or proposed a way forward. My student felt that her mother continued to find new ways to generate conflict with her. She asked if I had any other ideas for how she could make this better, or if there was something she might be missing.

Gently, I told her I thought she might be asking the wrong question—that perhaps this was not within her control at all. That perhaps her mother needed this conflict in some way, and was resisting efforts to solve or transform it. So maybe my student's work was to use the Mirror questions to identify her own needs and boundaries, and articulate those in order to keep herself safe.

All this to say: These questions presuppose certain conditions. They assume that the person on the other side is dealing in good faith. That the person does not have a personality disorder, or some reason why they need the conflict to exist. You will still get tremendous value from doing these questions, even in such a situation. For one thing, you will clarify your own sense of the problem—your needs, emotions, prior successes, and ideas for the future. Some of those steps may be within your control, and now you're on your way to achieving them. You will also have the satisfaction of knowing that you gave this conflict or issue a shot. You can't know until you try. And if you try and are not successful for one of the reasons I listed above, that is useful information to have. Now you can work toward achieving clarity on a different path forward, one that does not involve a partnership with the other person. In my student's case, she used these questions to articulate her needs and set a boundary with her mother. It isn't the relationship she dreamed of, but she feels safer and more accepting of the situation as it is.

Closing Thoughts

I wrote this book to bring you techniques that you can use to improve any negotiation or relationship in your life. And in doing so, improve your life itself.

They've certainly improved mine. When I first learned the skills you've read about in this book, I found that not only did I negotiate better, with myself and with others, but I felt a lot happier. I simultaneously felt more confident and more connected to the people around me. And then I used these skills to find my professional calling as a professor, mediator, and negotiation coach. Today and every day, I wake up knowing that I am doing what I was put on this earth to do. My purpose in writing this book was to help you do, and feel, the same. I love helping people reach their own personal highest and best, and then go on to share what they have learned with others.

In the course of writing this book, I've taken you along for some of the highs and lows of my life. In many ways, writing this book has felt like one long look in the Mirror. But I did this for a reason. I wrote this book from the Mirror so that you would feel free to negotiate from yours. I want you to know that when you go out to ask for more, you can do so as your full, authentic self. Not only is it okay, but you'll be most successful when you do.

When people complete negotiation training with me, even if just for a day, I tell them at the end that I consider them my new colleagues. What does that mean? It means you're now part of a community that is trying to "do good" in their negotiations even as they go out to achieve their goals. It means I want you to consider me your partner in your work from here on, to stay in touch, and tell me what you go on to do with what you have learned. And it means I hope you'll share some of what you've learned with others in your life. When you stay curious in your negotiations and relationships, you'll see that other people start looking to you as a model, and do the same. In this way, good negotiators become leaders—at home, at work, and in the world.

Ask for More: 10 Questions to Negotiate Anything

BY ALEXANDRA CARTER

THE MIRROR	THE WINDOW
My definition of the problem/goal: *What's the problem I want to solve?*	**Their definition of the problem/goal** *Tell me . . .*
My needs/what those look like *What do I need?*	**Their needs/what those look like** *What do you need?*
My feelings/concerns *What do I feel?*	**Their feelings/concerns** *What are your concerns?*
My previous success *How have I handled this successfully in the past?*	**Their previous success** *How have you handled this successfully in the past?*
My first steps *What's the first step?*	**Their first steps** *What's the first step?*

ACKNOWLEDGMENTS

This section was the hardest of any to write. From the moment I dreamed up the idea for this book to the moment of its publication, I have been lifted up by a huge community of family, friends, and colleagues. I owe everything to your support. Any errors are mine alone.

Profound thanks to Carol Liebman, my mentor, who first taught me to fish with a net, and to my community of dispute resolution colleagues across the country.

To my editor, Stephanie Frerich, who on our first phone call told me this was the negotiation book she'd been waiting for her whole professional life. You're the intellectual partner I've been waiting for all of mine. Thank you to my editing team at Simon & Schuster: editors Kimberly Goldstein and Annie Craig; publisher Jonathan Karp, and editor Emily Simonson. To my artistic team for helping me bring this book to visual and audible life: Lauren Pires, Jackie Seow, and Tom Spain. And to the rest of the team at Simon & Schuster that has enabled this book to empower people across the globe to ask for more: Kayley Hoffman, Alicia Brancato, Marie Florio, and Fritha Saunders.

To my agents, Esther Newberg and Kristyn Benton. I couldn't be prouder to be represented by you and by ICM Partners, an agency publicly committed to gender parity at all levels of management.

To my graduate, friend, and all-around inspiration, Kristen J. Ferguson, for holding up the mirror and helping me conceptualize this project.

If I gave birth to this book, you were my first midwife. Thank you for being the message.

To my colleagues at Columbia Law School, with special thanks to Dean Gillian Lester, Vice Dean Brett Dignam, and all my clinical faculty colleagues. Thank you to the entire Columbia Law School clinical administrative team: Brenda Eberhart, Michelle Ellis, Elizabeth Gloder, Mirlande Mersier, and Misty Swan. To those who generously spent time reading my book or offering advice and encouragement, including Elizabeth Emens, Michelle Greenberg-Kobrin, Avery Katz, Sarah Knuckey, Gillian Metzger, Colleen Shanahan, Susan Sturm, and Matthew Waxman. Thank you to my mentors, Robert Ferguson and Louis Henkin, for believing in me. I wish you were here to hold this book in your hands, but know that I am holding you in my heart. My mediation colleague for life, Shawn Watts, for more than I can capture here.

I teach the best students in the world. To my entire Columbia Law School student team, thank you for your ideas, edits, and your unfailing belief in this project: Jennifer Q. Ange, David S. Blackman, Argemira Flórez Feng, Heidi L. Guzmán, Xinrui Alex Li, Lauren Matlock-Colangelo, Ayisha Christen McHugh, Cecilia Plaza, Esther Portyansky, Dana M. Quinn, Shinji Ryu, and Nadia Yusuf. Special thanks to my book team "captains," Baldemar Gonzalez, Idun Bresee Klakegg, Kate Joohyun Lee, and Haley Ling, who were there from the beginning. Your expertise, your editorial input, and your hearts are reflected everywhere in this book.

To my family, for your support and advice. Special thanks to family authors Bill Carter and Caela Carter for paving the way. *Ask for More* is just the latest in the bookshelf of Carter volumes. My mother, Vera Carter, for being a role model in the classroom and in life. My father, Richard Carter, for teaching me grit and resilience. My bonus mom, Nikki Carter, for her encouragement. My beloved siblings: Rich and Brittany Carter, John and Katie Carter, Scott and Michelle Shepherd, and Henry Shepherd. My uncles and aunts: Elizabeth Keating Carter, Catherine and Daniel O'Neill, Alex and Wendy Ricci, and Dom Ricci. My awesome cousins, including Bridget, Christina, Dan, Danno, Jeannie, Mary Frances, and

Sabrina for their support on this project and in all my endeavors. My late grandparents, Richard and Teresa Carter, Frances and Tiberio Ricci, and Dick Regen. My wonderful in-laws: Tom and Regina Lembrich, Ellen Lembrich, and Dan Adshead.

To my close friends who have encouraged me throughout this and all my endeavors, including Dawn Behrmann, Paolo Bowyer, Jennifer Brick, Allison Ciechanover, Shoshana Eisenberg, Deborah Engel, Elyse Epstein, Ruth Hartman, Malia Rulon Herman, Meredith Katz, Reshma Ketkar, Lisa Landers, Marcia LeBeau, Marie McGehee, Laura Mummolo-Collins, Melanie Painvin, Dina Pressel, Rebecca Price, and Meghan Siket.

For stories, feedback, advice, comments and support, I am indebted to more people than I can capture here, including Kristy Bryce, Kate Buchanan, Autumn Calabrese, Julie China, Lisa Courtney, Ambassador Luis Gallegos, David Greenwald, Jamila Hall, Janet Stone Herman, Art Hinshaw, Kiley Holliday, Mila Jasey, Heather Kasdan, Bonnie Lau, Jodi Lipper, Shuva Mandal, Danielle and Celia Mann, Gabriel Matus, Ben McAdams, Julie Judd McAdams, Jamie Meier, Gray and Suzanne Sexton, Andra Shapiro, Ritu Sharma, Sherri Sparaga, George M. Soneff, Melody Tan, Mary Theroux, Anastasia Tsioulcas, Amy Walsh, Daniel Weitz, Elisha Wiesel, Hon. Mark L. Wolf, and Mei Xu.

To my colleagues at the United Nations and UNITAR: Assistant Secretary-General Nikhil Seth, Ambassador Marco Suazo, Pelayo Alvarez, Jones Haertle, Julia Maciel, and all of the hundreds of diplomats who have attended our courses and contributed to this book via their experiences.

To my friends and colleagues around the globe for their support. In Japan: Ambassador Ricardo Allicock, President Junko Hibiya of ICU, Michael Kawachi and family, and the rest of my Japan family. In Brazil: my mediation colleague, friend, and Brazilian sister, Professora Lilia Maia de Morais Sales and family; Professor Gustavo Feitosa; and my entire extended family at the University of Fortaleza, including the late Dr. Jose Airton Vidal Queiroz and President Fatima Veras.

To Mark Fortier and Melissa Connors, my publicists at Fortier Public

Relations, Kenneth Gillett and the team at Target Marketing Digital, as well as Brandi Bernoskie, Elsa Isaac, Tara Lauren, Gregory Patterson, and Rachel Zorel of 7 Layer Studio, for helping me bring this message to the world.

Every word of this book is brought to you by the superlative coffee and carbs found at Liv Breads in Millburn, New Jersey, owned by my friends Elana and Yaniv Livneh.

And to my home community of Maplewood, New Jersey, thank you for loving me and my family while I worked to bring this book into being.

NOTES

Introduction

1 **"by the depth of our answers":** Carl Sagan, *Cosmos* (New York: Random House, 1980), 193.

3 **only 7 percent of people ask good questions:** Leigh Thompson, *The Mind and Heart of the Negotiator* (New Jersey: Pearson/Prentice Hall, 2005), 77.

3 **you not only miss the chance:** Ibid.

4 **in a business or political situation:** "Negotiation," *Macmillan Dictionary*, October 2, 2019, https://www.macmillandictionary.com/us/dictionary/american/negotiation#targetText=formaldiscussionsinwhichpeople,contractnegotiations.

4 **try to reach an agreement:** "Negotiation," *Collins English Dictionary*, October 2, 2019, https://www.collinsdictionary.com/us/dictionary/english/negotiation.

7 **research on negotiation and leadership:** Tasha Eurich, *Insight: The Surprising Truth About How Others See Us, How We See Ourselves, and Why the Answers Matter More Than We Think* (New York: Random House, 2017), 99–101; Thompson, 77.

12 **Studies of the political and social climate:** James E. Campbell, *Polarized: Making Sense of a Divided America* (2016), 31; John Sides &

Daniel J. Hopkins, *Political Polarization in American Politics* (2015), 23.

12 **Research also demonstrates:** Wendy L. Bedwell, Stephen M. Fiore & Eduardo Salas, "Developing the Future Workforce: An Approach for Integrating Interpersonal Skills Into the MBA Classroom," *Academy of Management Learning and Communication* 13, no. 2 (2013): 172.

Part 1: The Mirror

16 **finds a decided link:** Tasha Eurich, *Insight: The Surprising Truth About How Others See Us, How We See Ourselves, and Why the Answers Matter More Than We Think* (New York: Random House, 2017), 154.

16 *two* **different kinds of self-awareness:** Ibid, 8.

16 **Internal self-awareness:** Ibid.

16 **External self-awareness:** Ibid.

16 **high external self-awareness but low internal self-awareness:** Ibid.

16 **worked on discovering how to increase self-awareness:** Ibid, 11–13

16 **accurate introspection depends on our asking:** Ibid, 101.

16 **exactly the *wrong* questions:** Ibid, 98–102.

16 **the question hanging heaviest:** Karen Zraick & David Scull, "Las Vegas, Puerto Rico, Tom Petty: Your Tuesday Evening Briefing," *New York Times*, October 3, 2017, https://www.nytimes .com/2017/10/03/briefing/las-vegas-donald-trump-puerto-rico-tom-petty.html.

17 **obtain higher levels of internal self-awareness:** Eurich, 100.

18 **proven to help us remember things better:** "Study Focuses on Strategies for Achieving Goals, Resolutions," Dominican University of California, October 2, 2019, https://www.dominican.edu/ dominicannews/study-highlights-strategies-for-achieving-goals.

18 **more likely to achieve them:** Mark Murphy, "Neuroscience Explains Why You Need to Write Down Your Goals if You Actually Want to Achieve Them," *Forbes*, April 15, 2018, https://www.forbes.com/sites/markmurphy/2018/04/15/neuroscience-explains-why-you-need-to-write-down-your-goals-if-you-actually-want-to-achieve-them/#40a5f44e7905.

One: What's the Problem I Want to Solve?

21 **five minutes thinking about solutions:** Erika Andersen, "Start the New Year Like Albert Einstein," *Forbes*, December 20, 2011, https://www.forbes.com/sites/erikaandersen/2011/12/30/start-the-new-year-like-albert-einstein/#6f3d58dd3e12.

21 **fresh off the success of the iPod, watched:** Fred Vogelstein, "The Untold Story: How the iPhone Blew Up the Wireless Industry," *Wired*, January 9, 2008, https://www.wired.com/2008/01/ff-iphone/.

21 **became less and less satisfied:** Mic Wright, "The Original iPhone Announcement Annotated: Steve Jobs' Genius Meets Genius," TNW, September 9, 2015, https://thenextweb.com/apple/2015/09/09/genius-annotated-with-genius/.

21 **burdened with a bunch of other devices:** Ibid.

21 **people needed one easy-to-use device:** Ibid.

22 **the only accessory it needed:** Ibid.

22 **set Apple's engineers to work:** Vogelstein, "The Untold Story: How the iPhone Blew Up the Wireless Industry."

22 **having negotiated a deal for their subsidiary:** Ibid.

22 **AT&T would have exclusive distribution rights:** Ibid.

22 **from each customer's wireless bill every month:** Ibid.

22 **Apple also retained control:** Ibid.

22 **never been seen before:** Ibid.

22 **told *Forbes* magazine:** Peter Cohan, "How Steve Jobs got ATT to Share Revenue," *Forbes*, August 16, 2013, https://www.forbes.com/

sites/petercohan/2013/08/16/how-steve-jobs-got-att-to-share-revenue/#527ef4f0391c.

22 **quickly captured a sizable segment:** "5 Years Later: A Look Back at the Rise of the iPhone," Comscore, June 29, 2012, https://www.comscore.com/Insights/Blog/5-Years-Later-A-Look-Back-at-the-Rise-of-the-iPhone.

22 **"For Jobs and the iPhone":** Kevin Ashton, "How to Fly a Horse: The Secret of Steve," October 2, 2019, http://howtoflyahorse.com/the-secret-of-steve/.

24 **10 percent or more of school days:** "The Problem," Attendance Works, Oct. 2, 2019, https://www.attendanceworks.org/chronic-absence/the-problem/.

24 **can translate into:** Ibid.

24 **According to non-profit Attendance Works:** Ibid.

25 **after combining the clothes-washing program:** Emily S. Rueb, "Schools Find a New Way to Combat Student Absences: Washing Machines," *New York Times*, Mar. 13, 2019, https://www.nytimes.com/2019/03/13/us/schools-laundry-rooms.html.

27 **"Creating is not a result of genius":** Ashton, "How to Fly a Horse: The Secret of Steve."

27 **"Twenty-five percent of failures were due to":** John Kennedy, "Darrell Mann: 98pc of Innovation Projects Fail, How to Be the 2pc that Don't," *Silicon Republic*, February 23, 2013, https://www.siliconrepublic.com/innovation/darrell-mann-98pc-of-innovation-projects-fail-how-to-be-the-2pc-that-dont.

28 **humans tend to avoid:** Erik van Mechelen, "Substituting a Hard Question for an Easier One: Daniel Kahneman's *Thinking, Fast and Slow*," *Yukaichou* (blog), October 2, 2019, https://yukaichou.com/behavioral-analysis/substituting-hard-question-easier-one-daniel-kahnemans-thinking-fast-thinking-slow/.

31 **the situation as it stands today:** Michael Cooper, "Defining Problems: The Most Important Business Skill You've Never Been

Taught," *Entrepreneur*, September 26, 2014, https://www.entrepreneur.com/article/237668.

31 **give you the clearest, most concise picture:** Ibid.

31 **achieve better results when you're focused on the goal:** Andrea Kupfer Schneider, "Aspirations in Negotiations," *Marquette Law Review* 87, no. 4 (2004): 675.

Two: What Do I Need?

40 **You'll know something is a need:** Sheiresa Ngo, "The Real Difference Between Needs and Wants Most People Ignore," Cheatsheet, November 6, 2017, https://www.cheatsheet.com/money-career/real-difference-between-needs-and-wants-people-ignore.html/.

40 **get more from their negotiations:** Sidney Siegel & Lawrence E. Fouraker, *Bargaining and Group Decision Making* (New York: McGraw-Hill, 1960), 64.

40 **"optimistic, specific, and justifiable":** G. Richard Shell, *Bargaining for Advantage: Negotiation Strategies for Reasonable People* (New York: Viking, 1999), 30–34.

40 **By identifying our needs:** Andrea Kupfer Schneider, "Aspirations in Negotiations," *Marquette Law Review* 87, no. 4 (2004): 676.

41 **helps us aspire to more:** Ibid, 34.

43 **Drawn from psychology research:** Abraham H. Maslow, "A Theory of Human Motivation," *Psychological Review* 50, no. 4 (1943): 394–395.

44 **"The link between hunger and conflict":** Edith M. Lederer, "UN: Conflict Key Cause of 124 Million Hungry Who Could Die," AP News, March 23, 2018, https://www.apnews.com/c37f7a8da9cc4e-aebf3fe7c48711aa37.

44 **"Conflict leads to food insecurity":** Ibid.

44 **"food insecurity can also stoke instability":** Ibid.

44 **60 percent of the 815 million:** Ibid.

47   **major determinant of both happiness and productivity:** Annie McKee, *How to Be Happy at Work: The Power of Purpose, Hope, and Friendship* (Boston: Harvard Business Review Press, 2018), 13.

47   **respect, which means admiration for someone:** "Respect," *Merriam-Webster*, October 16, 2019, https://www.merriam-webster.com/dictionary/respect.

47   **lack of respect in a partnership:** John Mordechai Gottman & Nan Silver, *The Seven Principles for Making Marriage Work* (New York: Random House, 1999), 29–31, 65–66.

47   **one of the "Four Horsemen" that predicts divorce:** Ibid., 27.

47   **more likely to give it in return:** Robert Cialdini, "The Six Principles of Successful Workplace Negotiation," Controlled Environments, September 4, 2015.

47   **Respect creates trust:** Ibid; Jeswald Salacuse, "The Importance of a Relationship in Negotiation," Program on Negotiation, Harvard Law School, June 18, 2019, https://www.pon.harvard.edu/daily/negotiation-training-daily/negotiate-relationships/.

47   **Dignity, which in some cultures is called "face":** Bert R. Brown, "Saving Face," *Psychology Today* 4, no. 12 (May 1971), 56–57.

47   **sense of pride and worthiness:** "Dignity," *Merriam-Webster*, October 16, 2019, https://www.merriam-webster.com/dictionary/dignity.

47   **critical to their well-being:** Jonathan M. Mann, "Dignity, Well-Being and Quality of Life," in *Longevity and Quality of Life: Opportunities and Challenges*, ed. Robert N Butler & Claude Jasmin (New York: Kluwer Academic, 2000), 149.

49   **need to know that they are in charge:** Roger Fisher & Daniel Shapiro, *Beyond Reason: Using Emotions as You Negotiate* (New York: Viking Penguin, 2005), 211.

49   **can help satisfy these self-direction needs:** Ibid; Sue Grossman, "Offering Children Choices: Encouraging Autonomy and Learning While Minimizing Conflicts," *Early Childhood News*, October 16, 2019, www.earlychildhoodnews.com/earlychildhood/article_view.aspx?ArticleID=607.

60 **"Life is a process of becoming"**: Evelyn J. Hinz, *The Mirror and the Garden: Realism and Reality in the Writings of Anaïs Nin* (1973), 40.

Three: What Do I Feel?

67 **our feelings help us make decisions:** Jim Camp, "Decisions are Largely Emotional, Not Logical: The Neuroscience Behind Decision-Making," Big Think, June 11, 2012, https://bigthink.com/experts-corner/decisions-are-emotional-not-logical-the-neuroscience-behind-decision-making.

67 **found that they were unable to make decisions:** Antonio Damasio, *Descartes' Error: Emotion, Reason, and the Human Brain* (New York: G.P. Putnam, 1994), 38-39, 50, 63.

67 **couldn't even decide what to eat:** Jonah Lehrer, "Feeling Our Way to Decision," *Sydney Morning Herald*, February 28, 2009, https://www.smh.com.au/national/feeling-our-way-to-decision-20090227-8k8v.html.

67 **can enhance our ability to judge:** Barbara L. Friedrickson, "What Good are Positive Emotions?," *Review of General Psychology* 2, no. 3 (1998): 300.

68 **can inhibit these abilities:** Christopher Bergland, "How Does Anxiety Short Circuit the Decision-Making Process?," *Psychology Today*, March 17, 2016, https://www.psychologytoday.com/us/blog/the-athletes-way/201603/how-does-anxiety-short-circuit-the-decision-making-process.

70 **in a way that impedes our ability:** Jessica J. Flynn, Tom Hollenstein & Allison Mackey, "The Effect of Suppressing and Not Accepting Emotions on Depressive Symptoms: Is Suppression Different for Men and Women?," *Personality and Individual Differences* 49, no. 6 (2010): 582.

74 **worked on devising groups of core emotions:** Brené Brown, "List of Core Emotions," March 2018, https://brenebrown.com/wp-content/uploads/2018/03/List-of-Core-Emotions-2018.pdf.

76 **"Let us never negotiate out of fear":** John F. Kennedy, "Inaugural Address," CNN, January 20, 1961, http://www.cnn.com/2011/POLITICS/01/20/kennedy.inaugural/index.html.

80 **have been shown to help build a connection:** Barbara Fredrickson, "Are you Getting Enough Positivity in Your Diet?," *Greater Good Magazine*, June 21, 2011, https://greatergood.berkeley.edu/article/item/are_you_getting_enough_positivity_in_your_diet

80 **you may experience more difficulty:** Meina Liu, "The Intrapersonal and Interpersonal Effects of Anger on Negotiation Strategies: A Cross-Cultural Investigation," *Human Communication Research* 35, no. 1 (2009): 148–69; Bo Shao, Lu Wang, David Cheng & Lorna Doucet, "Anger Suppression in Negotiations: The Roles of Attentional Focus and Anger Source," *Journal of Business & Psychology* 30, no. 4 (December 2015): 755.

80 **has been shown to lead to mixed results:** Program on Negotiation Staff, "Negotiation Strategies: Emotional Expression at the Bargaining Table," Harvard Law School Program on Negotiation: Daily Blog, June 6, 2019, https://www.pon.harvard.edu/daily/negotiation-skills-daily/emotional-expression-in-negotiation/.

80 **may be more likely to make concessions:** Jeff Falk-Rice, "In Negotiations, A Little Anger May Help," Futurity, March 15, 2018, https://www.futurity.org/anger-in-negotiations-emotions-1704482/.

80 **less likely to want to do business:** Keith G. Allred, John S. Mallozzi, Fusako Matsui & Christopher P. Raia, "The Influence of Anger and Compassion on Negotiation Performance," *Organizational Behavior and Human Decision Processes* 70, no. 3 (June 1997): 177.

80 **less power than your counterpart:** Mithu Storoni, "It Pays to Get Angry In a Negotiation—If You Do It Right," *Inc.*, May 11, 2017, https://www.inc.com/mithu-storoni/it-pays-to-get-angry-in-a-negotiation-if-you-do-it-right.html.

81 **Anxiety in negotiation can lead:** Alison Wood Brooks & Maurice E. Schweitzer, "Can Nervous Nelly Negotiate? How Anxiety

Causes Negotiators to Make Low First Offers, Exit Early, and Earn Less Profit," *Organizational Behavior and Human Decision Processes* 115, no. 1 (May 2011): 51.

Four: How Have I Handled This Successfully in the Past?

87   **more likely to achieve better results:** Joris Lammers, David Dubois, Derek D. Rucker & Adam D. Galinsky, "Power Gets the Job: Priming Power Improves Interview Outcomes," *Journal of Experimental Social Psychology* 49, no. 4 (July 2013): 778.

92   **One study at Columbia found:** Ibid.

92   **researchers at Harvard Business School found:** Kimberlyn Leary, Julianna Pillemer & Michael Wheeler, "Negotiating with Emotion," *Harvard Business Review*, January–February 2013, 96, 99, https://hbr.org/2013/01/negotiating-with-emotion.

92   **this effect is self-reinforcing:** Theresa Amabile & Steven Kramer, *The Progress Principle: Using Small Wins to Ignite Joy, Engagement, and Creativity at Work* (Boston: Harvard Business Review Press, 2011), 69.

92   **Says the *Harvard Business Review*:** Leary et al., "Negotiating with Emotion."

Five: What's the First Step?

99   **"close the gap between home and fashion":** Mei Xu, "Chesapeake Bay Candle: Mei Xu," interview by Guy Raz, *How I Built This*, NPR, March 6, 2017, Audio, 10:16, https://www.npr.org/2017/03/06/518132220/chesapeake-bay-candle-mei-xu.

99   **which she launched in 1994:** "Chesapeake Bay Candle," Newell Brands, October 10, 2019, https://www.newellbrands.com/our-brands/chesapeake-bay-candle.

107   **now-famous negotiation success story:** Brad McRae, *Negotiating and Influencing Skills: The Art of Creating and Claiming Value* (California: SAGE Publications, 1998), 19.

107   **planned for a whistle-stop trip:** Ibid.

107   **printed three million copies:** Ibid.

107   **they had not secured permission:** Ibid.

107   **they could be liable:** Ibid.

107   **couldn't afford the risk:** Ibid.

107   **came up with one:** Ibid.

107   **sent Moffett Studios the following cable:** Ibid.

107   **"We are planning to distribute":** Ibid.

107   **Moffett replied to the cable:** Ibid.

107   **They accepted:** Ibid.

107   **turned a potential liability:** Ibid.

111   **consider the worst-case scenario:** Ayse Birsel, "Your Worst Idea Might Be Your Best Idea," *Inc.*, February 16, 2017, https://www.inc.com/ayse-birsel/your-worst-idea-might-be-your-best-idea.html.

111   **just as well (or better) for negotiations that involve a group:** Ibid.

111–112   **some companies use this technique:** John Geraci, "Embracing Bad Ideas to Get to Good Ideas," *Harvard Business Review*, December 27, 2016, https://hbr.org/2016/12/embracing-bad-ideas-to-get-to-good-ideas.

112   **3M calls this "reverse thinking":** "Reverse Thinking: Turning the Problem Upside Down," Post-it, 3M, October 6, 2019, https://www.post-it.com/3M/en__US/post-it/ideas/articles/reverse-thinking/.

Part 2: The Window

115   **"When people talk, listen completely":** Ernest Hemingway, "Quotes," Goodreads, October 6, 2019, https://www.goodreads.com/quotes/1094622-when-people-talk-listen-completely-don-t-be-thinking-what-you-re.

115   **"Most people never listen":** Ibid.

115 **often fail to hear—or worse, actively devalue:** Will Tumonis, "How Reactive Devaluation Distorts Our Judgment," *Ideation Wiz*, December 17, 2014, https://www.ideationwiz.com/reactive-devaluation/.

116 **we are less than perfect listeners:** Ralph G. Nichols & Leonard A. Stevens, "Listening to People," *Harvard Business Review*, September 1957, https://hbr.org/1957/09/listening-to-people.

117 **93 percent of all negotiators failed to ask:** Leigh Thompson, *The Mind and Heart of the Negotiator* (Upper Saddle River, NJ: Pearson/Prentice Hall, 2005), 77.

118 **cluelessness, or a lack of strategic thinking, can result:** Michael Suk-Young Chwe, *Jane Austen, Game Theorist: Updated Edition* (Princeton, NJ: Princeton University Press, 2013), 188.

118 **empathic listeners not only create better connections:** Sharon Myers, "Empathic Listening: Reports on the Experience of Being Heard," *Journal of Humanistic Psychology* 40, no. 2 (2000): 171.

122 **when you listen in order to understand:** Stephen R. Covey, *The 7 Habits of Highly Effective People: Powerful Lessons in Personal Change* (New York: Simon & Schuster, 1989), 239–40.

123 **More than 50 percent of communication is non-verbal:** Allan & Barbara Pease, "The Definitive Book of Body Language," *New York Times*, September 24, 2006, https://www.nytimes.com/2006/09/24/books/chapters/0924-1st-peas.html; Albert Mehrabian: Silent Messages: Implicit Communication of Emotions and Attitudes (Belmont, CA: Wadsworth Publishing Co., 1981).

123 **"Even when you know a person well":** Chwe, *Jane Austen, Game Theorist: Updated Edition*, 17.

124 **"A person with good nunchi can understand":** Ibid.

124 **observe someone's default, or baseline:** Carol Kinsey Goman, "How to Read Business Body Language Like a Pro-5th Tip," *Forbes*, December 28, 2012, https://www.forbes.com/sites/carolkinseygoman/2012/12/28/how-to-read-business-body-language-like-a-pro-5th-tip/#54e7b7a463b5.

Six: Tell Me …

125 **a lifelong member of the Church of Latter-Day Saints:** Libby Coleman, "There's a Reason He's the Highest-Ranking Dem in Utah," Ozy, February 20, 2017, https://www.ozy.com/politics-and-power/theres-a-reason-hes-the-highest-ranking-dem-in-utah/75784.

125 **is a first-time United States congressperson:** Lee Davidson, "It's Over. Democrat Ben McAdams Ousts Republican Rep. Mia Love by 694 Votes," *Salt Lake Tribune*, November 21, 2018, https://www.sltrib.com/news/politics/2018/11/20/its-over-democrat-ben/.

125 **unusual for a practicing Mormon:** Coleman, "There's a Reason He's the Highest-Ranking Dem in Utah."

125 **has spent much of his adult life:** Ibid.

125 **One day in 2008:** Jared Page, "Ben McAdams Quiets Critics with Willingness to Listen, Compromise," *Deseret News*, August 12, 2012, https://www.deseretnews.com/article/865560557/Ben-McAdams-quiets-critics-with-willingness-to-listen-compromise.html.

125 **2008, the year in which the Mormon Church:** Jesse McKinley & Kirk Johnson, "Mormons Tipped Scale in Ban on Gay Marriage," *New York Times*, November 14, 2008, https://www.nytimes.com/2008/11/15/us/politics/15marriage.html.

125 **proposed a "Domestic-Partnership Registry:** Page, "Ben McAdams Quiets Critics with Willingness to Listen, Compromise."

126 **including from within McAdams's own religion:** Page; "Buttars Shames LDS Church," *Deseret News*, January 30, 2006, https://www.deseret.com/2006/1/30/19935132/buttars-shames-lds-church.

126 **resisted the ordinance:** Ibid.

126 **to set up a meeting:** Ibid.

126 **"I usually find that when I listen":** Ibid.

126 **led to the creation of Salt Lake City's Mutual Commitment Registry:** Ibid.

126 **modified ordinance was unanimously approved:** Ibid.

126 **Julie (herself a trained mediator), later told:** Ibid.

127 **"wellsprings of innovation":** Alison Wood Brooks & Leslie K. John, "The Surprising Power of Questions," *Harvard Business Review*, May–June 2018, 60, 64, https://hbr.org/2018/05/the-surprising-power-of-questions.

128 **have called a "learning conversation":** Douglas Stone, Bruce Patton & Sheila Heen, *Difficult Conversations* (New York: Penguin Books, 2010), 16–20.

128 **an elected member and Deputy Speaker:** "Assemblywoman Mila Jasey Named Deputy Speaker of General Assembly," *The Village Green*, September 22, 2016, https://villagegreennj.com/towns/assemblywoman-mila-jasey-named-deputy-speaker-general-assembly/.

128 **won an important legislative battle on a divisive issue:** "NJSBA Applauds End of Unnecessary Superintendent Salary CAP," New Jersey School Boards Association, July 20, 2019, https://www.njsba.org/news-publications/press-releases/njsba-applauds-end-of-unnecessary-superintendent-salary-cap/.

128 **had instituted a salary cap for superintendents:** Joe Hernandez, "N.J. Considers Eliminating Cap on Superintendent Pay," Whyy, June 10, 2019, https://whyy.org/articles/n-j-considers-eliminating-cap-on-superintendent-pay/.

130 **"Tell me about yourself" is the only ice-breaker you need:** Jolie Kerr, "How to Talk to People, According to Terry Gross," *New York Times*, November 17, 2018, https://www.nytimes.com/2018/11/17/style/self-care/terry-gross-conversation-advice.html.

131 **"The beauty in opening with 'tell me about yourself'":** Ibid.

Seven: What Do You Need?

143 **needs, not rights, are the real reason:** Charles Vincent, Magi Young & Angela Phillips, "Why Do People Sue Doctors? A Study of Patients And Relatives Taking Legal Action," *The Lancet* 343, no. 8913 (June 1994): 1611–13.

147 **yields deep-seated, important information:** Katie Shonk, "Principled Negotiation: Focus on Interests to Create Value," Program on Negotiation, Harvard Law School, May 9, 2019, https://www.pon .harvard.edu/daily/negotiation-skills-daily/principled-negotiation-focus-interests-create-value/; Douglas Stone, Bruce Patton & Sheila Heen, *Difficult Conversations* (Penguin Books, 2010), 210–216.

150 **Social workers rarely ask *why* questions:** "Interviewing Skill Development and Practice," *Georgia Division of Family and Children Services*, March 2007, 10, dfcs.dhr.georgia.gov/sites/dfcs.georgia .gov/files/imported/DHR-DFCS/DHR_DFCS-Edu/Files/PG_ intermediate%20interviewing_rev03-07.pdf.

Eight: What Are Your Concerns?

156 **information that will be critical:** Caroline Cenzia-Levine, "Stuck in a Negotiation? Five Steps to Take when You Hear No to Your Request," *Forbes*, August 12, 2018, https://www.forbes.com/sites/ carolinecenizalevine/2018/08/12/stuck-in-a-negotiation-five-steps-to-take-when-you-hear-no-to-your-request/#69a7aea2737c.

158 **is that it builds rapport:** PON Staff, "Negotiating Skills: Learn How to Build Trust at the Negotiation Table," *Program on Negotiation, Harvard Law School*, September 9, 2019, https://www.pon .harvard.edu/daily/dealmaking-daily/dealmaking-negotiations-how-to-build-trust-at-the-bargaining-table/; Ilana Zohar, "'The Art of Negotiation': Leadership Skills Required for Negotiation in Time of Crisis," *Procedia - Social and Behavioral Sciences* 209 (July 2015): 542.

159 **how critical feelings are to unlocking conflict:** Alison Wood Brooks, "Emotion and the Art of Negotiation," *Harvard Business Review*, December 2015, https://hbr.org/2015/12/emotion-and-the-art-of-negotiation?referral=00060.

Nine: How Have You Handled This Successfully in the Past?

169   **expand our pie of potential options:** Paul E. Smaldino & Peter J. Richerson, "The Origins of Options," *Frontiers in Neuroscience*, April 11, 2012, https://www.frontiersin.org/articles/10.3389/fnins.2012.00050/full.

169   **memory influences how we make decisions:** Ibid.

169   **influence our sense of motivation and empowerment:** Joris Lammers, David Dubois, Derek D. Rucker & Adam D. Galinsky, "Power Gets the Job: Priming Power Improves Interview Outcomes," *Journal of Experimental Social Psychology* 49, no. 4 (2013): 778.

169   **research has shown to improve:** Ibid.

170   **remember concrete strategies that might help:** Smaldino & Richerson, "The Origins of Options."

171   **"power priming":** Lammers, Dubois, Rucker & Galinsky, "Power Gets the Job: Priming Power Improves Interview Outcomes," *Journal of Experimental Social Psychology* 49, no. 4 (2013): 778.

171   **"coax[ing] ourselves into feeling more or less powerful":** "Business School Professor Explores the Effects of Power," *Columbia News*, June 28, 2013, https://news.columbia.edu/news/business-school-professor-explores-effects-power.

171   **Hundreds of studies have shown:** Ibid.

171–172   **can produce the same effects as actually having power:** Pamela K. Smith & Yaacov Trope, "You Focus on the Forest When You're in Charge of the Trees: Power Priming and Abstract Information Processing," *Journal of Personality and Social Psychology* 90, no. 4 (2006): 580 ("Priming power should function in the same manner as actually experiencing it. Like any other concept, power is linked in memory to a host of characteristics and behavioral tendencies.").

172   **like in negotiation:** Alain P.C.I. Hong & Per J. van der Wijst, "Women in Negotiation: Effects of Gender and Power on Negotiation Behavior," *Negotiation and Conflict Management Research,*

International Association for Conflict Management 6, no. 4 (2013): 281.

174 **more likely to perform better:** PON Staff, "Power in Negotiation: The Impact on Negotiators and the Negotiation Process," *Program on Negotiation, Harvard Law School*, July 25, 2019, https://www .pon.harvard.edu/daily/negotiation-skills-daily/how-power-af-fects-negotiators/.

Ten: What's the First Step?

179 **David Greenwald led his firm—Fried, Frank:** Meghan Tribe, "Fried Frank Keeps Up Growth, Doubling Partner Profits over Five-Year Span," *The American Lawyer*, March 21, 2019, https:// www.law.com/americanlawyer/2019/03/21/fried-frank-keeps-up-growth-doubling-partner-profits-over-five-year-span/.

179 **he found a number of pressing issues:** Leigh McMullan Abramson, "Top Goldman Lawyer Helped Turn Around a Struggling Law Firm," *Big Law Business*, July 15, 2016, https:// biglawbusiness.com/top-goldman-lawyer-helped-turn-around-a-struggling-law-firm.

179 **comprise the majority of the firm's lawyers:** "The Responsibility Factor, AKA the Partner-Associate Ratio," Chambers Associate, October 10, 2019, https://www.chambers-associate.com/law-firms/partner-associate-leverage.

180 **ranks the nation's biggest law firms:** "Surveys & Rankings," *The American Lawyer*, October 10, 2019, https://www.law.com/ameri-canlawyer/rankings/.

180 **satisfaction of their mid-level associates:** ALM Staff, "Which Firms Keep Midlevel Associates Happiest? The 2019 National Rankings," *The American Lawyer*, August 26, 2019, https://www .law.com/americanlawyer/2019/08/26/where-are-midlevel-associ-ates-happiest-the-2019-national-rankings/.overall.

180 **satisfaction ranking takes into account:** Ibid.

180 **Fried Frank's associate satisfaction ranking was 132:** "The 2013 Associate Survey: National Rankings," *The American Lawyer*, September 1, 2013, https://www.law.com/americanlawyer/almID/1202614824184/.

180 **law firms generally have a lot of turnover:** Sam Reisman, "Turnover High At Many Firms Despite Greater Pay, Benefits," *Law360*, October 18, 2017, https://www.law360.com/articles/975882/turnover-high-at-many-firms-despite-greater-pay-benefits.

180 **established twice-yearly town hall meetings:** Dearbail Jordan, "How to Revive a Law Firm," *The Lawyer*, December 5, 2016, https://www.friedfrank.com/files/PressHighlights/TL%20-%20Feature%20Fried%20Frank%20-%20reprint.pdf

181 **met regularly with a smaller associate committee:** Ibid.

181 **surveyed associates again:** "The Best Places to Work," *The American Lawyer*, August 24, 2015, https://www.law.com/americanlawyer/almID/1202735469012/.

181 **satisfaction ranking jumped:** Ibid.

181 **landing them at #8:** MP McQueen, "Survey: Midlevel Associates are Happier Than Ever," *The American Lawyer*, September 1, 2016, https://www.law.com/americanlawyer/almID/1202765213979/Survey-Midlevel-Associates-Are-Happier-Than-Ever/.

182 **financial results have turned around:** Tribe, "Fried Frank Keeps Up Growth, Doubling Partner Profits over Five-Year Span."

182 **passed the $3 million mark:** Ibid.

183 **people tend to reciprocate gestures in negotiation:** Robert Cialdini, "The Six Principles of Successful Workplace Negotiation," Controlled Environments, September 4, 2015.

183 **you're more likely to get them to do it:** Ibid.

183 **sense of purpose, which makes them happier:** Annie McKee, "The 3 Things You Need to Be Happy at Work," *Annie McKee*, September 5, 2017, www.anniemckee.com/3-things-need-happy-work/.

183 **what Stanford psychologist Carol Dweck calls a "growth**

mind-set": Carol S. Dweck, *Mindset: The New Psychology of Success* (New York: Random House, 2006), 7.

183 **embarked on a study:** Corinne Purtill, "Exactly How Many Bad Ideas Does It Take to Produce a Good One? One Scientist Tried to Find Out," *Quartz*, Aug. 30, 2017, https://qz.com/1062945/the-value-of-bad-ideas-according-to-a-scientist/.

183 **had had a lot of success for a medical academic:** Ibid.

183 **many of his ideas failed:** Ibid.

183 **75 percent of the 185 ideas he found:** Ibid.

183 **only 2.7 percent of his ideas met his criteria:** Ibid.

184 **"The issue here is to recognize":** Ibid.

184 **"You cannot tell initially":** Ibid.

184 **improves patient compliance with treatment:** Kelly B. Haskard Zolnierek & M. Robin DiMatteo, Physician Communication and Patient Adherence to Treatment: A Meta-Analysis, *Medical Care* 47, no. 8 (August 2009): 826–834.

184 **"The medical profession is no longer":** Dhruv Khullar, "Teaching Doctors the Art of Negotiation," *New York Times*, January 23, 2014, https://well.blogs.nytimes.com/2014/01/23/teaching-doctors-the-art-of-negotiation/.

184 **"Rather, clinicians and patients deliberate":** Ibid.

184 **not only feel more satisfaction:** Ibid.

185 **asking the patient to participate in deciding the course of treatment:** Floyd J. Fowler Jr., Carrie A. Levin & Karen R. Sepucha, "Informing and Involving Patients to Improve the Quality of Medical Decisions," *Health Affairs* 30, no. 4 (2011): 699–700.

185 **presenting the list of possible options to the patient:** "Strategy 6I: Shared Decisionmaking," *Agency for Healthcare Research and Quality*, October 2017, https://www.ahrq.gov/cahps/quality-improvement/improvement-guide/6-strategies-for-improving/communication/strategy6i-shared-decisionmaking.html#ref8.

185 **increasing the patient's adherence:** Zolnierek & DiMatteo;

National Business Coalition on Health, "NBCH Action Brief: Shared Decision Making," Patient-Centered Primary Care Coalition, July 2012, https://www.pcpcc.org/sites/default/files/resources/ NBCH_AB_DECISIONMAKING_C.pdf.

185 **improves statistics while creating savings:** Ibid; Elizabeth C. Devine & Thomas D. Cook, "A Meta-Analytic Analysis of Effects of Psychoeducational Interventions on Length of Postsurgical Hospital Stay," *Nursing Research* 32, no. 5 (1983): 267.

185 **non-compliance with treatment is estimated to cost billions:** Brian Fung, "The $289 Billion Cost of Medication Noncompliance, and What to Do About It," *The Atlantic*, September 11, 2012, https://www.theatlantic.com/health/archive/2012/09/the-289-billion-cost-of-medication-noncompliance-and-what-to-do-about-it/262222/.

185 **feeling of connection with their coworkers:** Annie McKee, *How to Be Happy at Work: The Power of Purpose, Hope, and Friendship* (Boston: Harvard Business Review Press, 2018), 9.

185 **what leads to healthy personal relationships:** Bhali Gill, "Empathy is Crucial to Any Personal or Professional Relationship— Here's How to Cultivate It," *Forbes*, November 17, 2017, https:// www.forbes.com/sites/bhaligill/2017/11/17/empathy-is-crucial-to-any-personal-or-professional-relationship-heres-how-to-cultivate-it/#73b0f3ae7961; Masoumeh Tehrani-Javan, Sara Pashang & Maryam Mashayekh, "Investigating the Empathy Relationship and Interpersonal Relationships Quality Among Senior Managers," *Journal of Psychology & Behavioral Studies* 4, no. 1 (2016): 17.

186 **went to the Mayo Clinic for evaluation:** Sharing Mayo Clinic, "After Back Surgery, Jamie Ruden's on the Court Again and Looking to Help Others," Mayo Clinic, July 31, 2019, https://sharing .mayoclinic.org/2019/07/31/after-back-surgery-jamie-rudens-on-the-court-again-and-looking-to-help-others/.

186 **knew there were a couple of possible solutions:** Ibid.

187 **The doctor asked the patient:** Ibid.

187 **She felt that the conservative approach:** Ibid.

187 **The doctor supported that choice:** Ibid.

187 **committed to working hard:** Ibid.

187 **she later told the Mayo Clinic:** Ibid.

187 **Jamie opted for the surgery:** Ibid.

187 **helped, but didn't eliminate:** Ibid.

187 **helped Jamie and her family:** Ibid.

187 **The surgery was successful:** Ibid.

191 **group brainstorming:** Alex Faickney Osborn, *Principles and Procedures of Creative Writing* (New York: Scribner, 1957), 228–229.

191 **would produce the best, most innovative results:** Ibid.

191 **shows that group brainstorming often doesn't work:** Donald W. Taylor, Paul C. Berry & Clifford H. Block, "Does Group Participation When Using Brainstorming Facilitate or Inhibit Creative Thinking?," *Administrative Science Quarterly* 3, no. 1 (June 1958): 43.

191 **Individual work that then gets honed in a group:** Marvin D. Dunnette, John Campbell & Kay Jaastad, "The Effect of Group Participation on Brainstorming Effectiveness for 2 Industrial Samples," *Journal of Applied Psychology* 47, no. 1 (1963): 36–37.

Bring It Home: Concluding Your Negotiation

196 **aspirations are based on our needs:** Andrea Kupfer Schneider, "Aspirations in Negotiations," *Marquette Law Review* 87, no. 4 (2004): 676.

196 **make sure your aspirations are justifiable:** G. Richard Shell, *Bargaining for Advantage: Negotiation Strategies for Reasonable People* (New York: Viking, 1999), 30–34.

196 **tie your asks to anything objective:** Roger Fisher, William Ury &

Bruce Patton, *Getting to Yes: Negotiating Agreement Without Giving In* (New York: Houghton Mifflin, 1991), 88.

198 **human beings are very loss-avoidant:** Daniel Kahneman, Jack L. Knetsch & Richard H. Thaler, "Experimental Tests of the Endowment Effect and the Coase Theorem," *Journal of Political Economy* 98, no. 6 (Dec. 1990): 1328.

INDEX

ABOUT THE AUTHOR

ALEXANDRA CARTER is a clinical professor of law and director of the Mediation Clinic at Columbia Law School. She is a negotiation trainer for the United Nations, as well as for Fortune 500 companies, government agencies, non-profits, and more. Carter graduated with honors from Georgetown University, was a Fulbright Scholar in Taiwan, and received her law degree from Columbia Law School. In 2019, Carter was awarded Columbia University's highest teaching honor. She lives in Maplewood, New Jersey, with her husband and daughter.